Developing Inclusive Practice for Young Children with Fetal Alcohol Spectrum Disorders

A Framework of Knowledge and Understanding for the Early Childhood Workforce

Carolyn Blackburn

Routledge
Taylor & Francis Group

LONDON AND NEW YORK

First published 2017
by Routledge
2 Park Square, Milton Park, Abingdon, Oxon OX14 4RN

and by Routledge
711 Third Avenue, New York, NY 10017

Routledge is an imprint of the Taylor & Francis Group, an informa business

British Library Cataloguing in Publication Data
A catalogue record for this book is available from the British Library

Library of Congress Cataloging in Publication Data
A catalog record for this book has been requested

ISBN: 978-1-138-83930-4 (hbk)
ISBN: 978-1-138-83932-8 (pbk)
ISBN: 978-1-315-73350-0 (ebk)

Typeset in Sabon
by Taylor & Francis Books

Contents

Foreword   vii

Acknowledgements   ix

1 Introduction: The role of teratogens in children's development   1

2 Fetal Alcohol Spectrum Disorders   7

3 Policy for early childhood inclusion and intervention   21

4 Theory, assessment, pedagogy and support   35

5 Framework of knowledge and understanding to support young children
   prenatally exposed to alcohol/diagnosed with FASD   51

6 Making human beings human: Relationship-based early childhood inclusion
   and intervention   59

Appendix A: Sensory preferences profile   66
Appendix B: Sensory passport   70
References   78
Index   85

Foreword

The World Health Organization describes Fetal Alcohol Spectrum Disorder (FASD) as a 'time-bomb ticking'. This timely book may help us diffuse that time bomb before it explodes! Carolyn Blackburn brings all of her experiences as an early childhood professional and researcher to bear in illuminating just how destructive to fetal development alcohol is, and how prenatal exposure to alcohol can significantly alter the developmental trajectory of children. The whole thrust of this text powerfully reminds us that FASD is 100% preventable, and 100% irreversible.

Years of research in the field of Early Childhood Intervention (Guralnick, 2005) has clearly demonstrated the benefits to children and families of early, timely and individually tailored support. However, lack of professional knowledge about FASD, the bio-psychosocial ramifications and the implications of the compromised learning pathways, mean that interventions may not be designed to embrace young children with FASD as active learners engaged in a stimulating environment that can aid and promote their development in all domains. To shape high-quality practice in the future, professionals deserve to have their pathway of development illuminated and articulated. The wealth of information presented in chapters on policy, evidence-based practice, support and intervention in this book do just that.

Carefully crafted text, littered with case studies, aids the readers' understanding of who this child is, their likely prior experiences, and how, with skilful support, nurture and care their development can be optimised throughout early childhood inclusion and intervention. Children's experiences even after the toxicity and commensurate trauma of the prenatal period are not without further potentially negative episodes. Some children may lose or be removed from their biological family. They may find themselves in multiple foster care placements. This will impact on bonding, nurturing and attachment.

In an early childhood setting there is the risk that the child may become withdrawn, agitated or develop unusual attachment relationships which need additional support. How will they communicate if they are overwhelmed by feelings of insecurity? Will they find learning too challenging as they try to regulate their emotional state? Or become nervous and anxious in a busy, fast-moving setting – an anxious child is not a learning child.

The strength of this book lies in the fact that it keeps the child as its central focus; at the heart of its debate, pulling on perspectives from research across a variety of disciplines and internationally, and from evidence-based practice from an array of interdisciplinary perspectives. The family-centred approach adopted throughout the book wraps around the child, whether that be from the biological family, the foster carer, or adoptive family.

Carolyn Blackburn has opened a window of professional opportunity for early childhood professionals through the information, knowledge and insight she offers in this book. Couched in the language of early childhood, clearly set in the context of those early years, the reader is invited to embark on a journey for and with the child with FASD. Through powerful and illuminative discussions around policy, theory, pedagogy and support, this book certainly achieves its aim of introducing a framework of knowledge and understanding as a tool to develop inclusive practice for young children prenatally exposed to alcohol.

It does so with creativity, care and compassion.

Professor Barry Carpenter, CBE

Acknowledgements

I would like to dedicate this book to all of the children and young people with Fetal Alcohol Spectrum Disorders whom I have had the pleasure to meet and work with in educational settings, and the families they live with who have shared their stories with me over the last fifteen years.

Further thanks to the professionals who strive continually to improve their inclusive practice to support children in the best way possible.

Not least, sincere thanks to all of the charities (mostly run by parents of children with FASD themselves) that tirelessly campaign for the rights of children, young people and adults with FASD.

This book would not have been possible without the support of Alison Foyle and her colleagues at Routledge Education.

My knowledge about FASD has grown from my professional friendship with Dr Raja Mukherjee, Professor Barry Carpenter and Jo Egerton, and the opportunities I have had to share the lives of children, families and professionals.

Chapter 1

Introduction

The role of teratogens in children's development

Introduction

The purpose of this chapter is to explain the position of this book in the early childhood workforce and explain the context. Early childhood professionals (ECPs) are trained and skilled to focus on the strengths and interests of individual children. This book adopts a relational, bio-psychosocial approach to understanding the effects of prenatal exposure to alcohol. It aims to provide ECPs with a framework of knowledge and understanding as a tool to develop inclusive practice to support children and families in a sensitive, respectful manner. This takes account of the complex and compounding sociocultural/sociohistorical and political factors that need to be considered for children exposed to alcohol prenatally.

Why is this book needed?

Early child development is influenced by factors such as early infant-caregiver relationships, cognitive and language stimulation, nutrition, and safe and healthy environments as well as the child's own genetic inheritance (Whitebread and Bingham, 2011). Genes and experiences interact to determine an individual's vulnerability to early adversity. For children experiencing severe adversity, environmental influences can be at least as, if not more powerful than genetic predispositions in their impact on the odds of having health problems and disabilities later in life.

The influence of maternal health and well-being is significant in children's development. In particular, maternal alcohol consumption is known to result in a variety of birth anomalies for infants which lie on a continuum from mild to profound and can evolve and become more pronounced as children mature, limiting children's participation in a range of educational and social settings (Streissguth and Kanter, 1997; Kleinfeld and Westcott, 1993; Karr-Morse and Wiley, 1997; Blackburn et al., 2012). Alcohol is one of many teratogens, the most famous of which is the drug thalidomide (Lenz, 1988), which caused a number of birth defects in infants exposed to the drug whose mothers took it in good faith that it was safe.

Teratogens

A teratogen is a substance that interferes with the normal development of the embryo or fetus. Examples include both illegal substances and those that we can buy over the counter or take for granted as a basic 'food stuff' such as alcohol. A wider discussion about the short- and long-term effects of a wide range of teratogens can be found elsewhere (for example, Murphy Paul, 2010; Chasnoff, 2010; and Karr-Morse and Wiley, 1997). Examples include:

- Drugs (for example, prescribed penicillin, diet pills, vitamin A)
- Tobacco
- Illegal drugs (cocaine, heroin)
- Alcohol
- Lead, mercury, solvents and other environmental pollutants
- Maternal diseases (for example, cancer, toxoplasmosis, chickenpox, tuberculosis)
- Herbal medications
- Extreme maternal stress.

For some of these substances, the full effects on a fetus are not known; for example, herbal medications have not been tested on pregnant women for ethical reasons. Illegal drugs and tobacco, by contrast, are known to place the developing fetus at risk of a range of neurobehavioural and learning difficulties for children, not to mention increasing the risk of miscarriage and premature birth (Shonkoff, 2010).

When educators (and other professionals) are asked about the least and most harmful of the above substances, it is the author's experience that many educators will mention illegal drugs or environmental pollutants such as lead and mercury as the most harmful. In fact alcohol is known to present the most serious risk to a developing fetus (Institute of Medicine, 1996). The effects of alcohol on the behaviour of a developing fetus can be measured *in utero* and have been shown to exert adverse impacts on normal neurobehavioural processes, contributing to the adverse consequences seen after birth. In addition, prenatal exposure to alcohol (PEA) may prime the individual to prefer alcohol after birth (Hepper, 2013). Collectively the range of effects of PEA has been termed Fetal Alcohol Spectrum Disorders (FASD). Children with FASD have diverse and complex learning difficulties and disabilities as demonstrated by the inclusion of FASD in the Complex Learning Difficulties and Disabilities Project, funded by the UK Department for Education (Carpenter et al., 2015). However, many children who experience PEA are not diagnosed with FASD, as is discussed in the next chapter. They may, however, be diagnosed with other conditions as discussed below.

The range of effects that arise from PEA are illustrated by the recent finding from Popova and colleagues (2016) that of 127 studies that met eligibility criteria from a systematic literature search, 428 identified co-existing conditions were found to co-occur in individuals with FASD. The most prevalent disease conditions were within the sections of the literature search on congenital malformations, deformities, chromosomal abnormalities, and mental and behavioural disorders. Some 33 studies reported data for frequency in a total of 1,728 participants with FASD. The five co-existing conditions with the highest pooled prevalence (between 50% and 91%) included abnormal results of function studies of peripheral nervous system and special senses, conduct disorder, receptive language disorder, chronic serous otitis media, and expressive language disorder. The authors concluded that the high prevalence of co-existing conditions in individuals with FASD highlights the importance of assessing prenatal alcohol exposure as a substantial clinical risk factor for co-existence. The harmful effects of alcohol on a developing fetus represent many cases of preventable disability, and thus, alcohol use during pregnancy should be recognised as a public health problem globally. Further to this, Young, Absoud, Blackburn and colleagues (2016: 5) recommended that if a child has been previously diagnosed with attention deficit hyperactivity disorder (ADHD) then the clinician should routinely screen for FASD and likewise FASD for ADHD, and clinicians should refer for multimodal assessments (often involving parents, teachers, occupational therapists, and speech and language therapists), when necessary, to assist them in treatment plan development.

Not enough is known about maternal risk in relation to FASD as currently we cannot predict risk (Mukherjee et al., 2005). However, risk has been described as 'multidimensional' (May and Gossage, 2011) and to include factors related to quantity, frequency and timing of alcohol exposure; maternal age; number of pregnancies; number of times the mother has given birth; the mother's body size; nutrition; socioeconomic status (SES); metabolism; religion; spirituality; depression; other drug use; and social relationships. In particular low socioeconomic status, under-nutrition, advanced maternal age, high parity, and overall weathering (the cumulative effect of poor living conditions, inadequate nutrition and high levels of stress on childbearing) are reported to increase the risk for FASD trait expression (Abel and Hannigan, 1995).

More research is needed to define more clearly what type of individual behavioural, physical and genetic factors are most likely to lead to having children with FASD (May and Gossage, 2011). However, animal research has shown that the genetic profiles of both the mother and fetus are important for determining the potential for risk of prenatal mortality, alcohol-related physical birth defects, and learning and other neurobehavioural problems in children (Warren et al., 2011). Further risks from prenatal alcohol exposure include prematurity of birth, low birth weight, and birth complications. A recent study exploring the role of epigenetics in neurodevelopmental disorders found that prenatal alcohol exposure is associated with distinct DNA methylation[1] patterns in children and adolescents, raising the possibility of an epigenetic[2] biomarker of FASD (Portales-Casamar et al., 2016).

For some children, maternal alcohol consumption represents a risk in addition to pre-existing biological, genetic and/or psychosocial influences, such as psychological trauma, impoverished environment, rendering them vulnerable to a toxic cocktail of risk factors. Such children have a biological or genetic predisposition to experience learning, social and/or behavioural difficulties which are not ameliorated by a supportive, nurturing environment conducive to the development of healthy attachments and relationships with others. Parent-child attachments are dependent on mutually reciprocal inter-subjective interactions between caregiver and child, and are crucial for the healthy development of children's social, emotional, cognitive and language development. This is sometimes difficult to achieve when infants are irritable, cry persistently, are difficult to feed and have poor sleep patterns, which are common difficulties for children with FASD. It is exacerbated when caregivers experience mental-ill health, inadequate coping strategies, insensitive parenting skills or substance addiction or dependency, for example:

> When I was pregnant I couldn't get up in the morning without throwing up and having a drink and I knew that I shouldn't, but I couldn't function without a drink … mentally I was unfit, I had suicidal thoughts, and I had thoughts about harming my son, was seeing things, I was a mess. Having a baby and trying to deal with my head was difficult.
>
> (Anonymous birth mother, Blackburn, 2013: 106)

Lack of healthy attachments may add to parental stress factors, adding further risk to development. Consequently, these children may lack the resilience that would help them to overcome life challenges. Societies and communities that fail to understand the complex transactional interplay between the impact of the cumulative effects of this toxic mix on the development of individual children and the quality of the human environment and communities that these children inhabit are failing in their responsibility to these children. They are also participating in their own destruction. Such children are vulnerable to exhibiting violent, aggressive and criminal behaviour in later life (Karr-Morse, 1997: 12).

The literature on neuroscience (Goswami, 2008) and early childhood intervention (ECI) (Guralnick, 2005) notes that early identification of any child at risk of developmental delays and difficulties, when supported with subsequent intervention, results in significant gains in children's development. ECI can improve opportunities for social inclusion, participation and the development of key life skills and independence, which benefit longer-term outcomes such as education and employment.

In the absence of inclusion and participation, as children mature they can become isolated and insular (Egerton, 2013). Children's rights to early childhood inclusion are embodied within the United Nations Convention on the Rights of the Child (1989) and Convention on the Rights of Persons with Disabilities (2006). These have been incorporated into the UK Special Educational Needs Code of Practice (Department for Education and Department of Health, 2015) and the *Children and Families Act* (2014), and these will be returned to later in the book. Inclusive practice underpins the principles of the Early Years Foundation Stage (EYFS) (DfE, 2014).

What is the role of early childhood professionals?

In order to effectively develop inclusive practice for children with FASD, ECPs must be equipped with sufficient knowledge and information.

In a study conducted in the UK (2009) 78% of early childhood professionals (164 participants) reported that they knew little or nothing about FASD and therefore would have found it difficult to plan for and support a child with FASD attending their early childhood setting (Blackburn and Whitehurst, 2010: 125). This study included Early Childhood Leaders in Sure Start[3] Children's Centres where one practitioner admitted honestly that she felt 'ignorant to work in a Children's Centre and not know about something like this [FASD]' (Blackburn and Whitehurst, 2010: 126). In a more recent study, conducted in Western Australia (Frances, 2013), of 236 early childhood professionals, the majority of participants had a high level of awareness of the effects of maternal alcohol consumption during pregnancy on the developing fetus but did not believe they had the appropriate skills and knowledge to support children with FASD.

This paucity of knowledge transcends different disciplines for those professionals involved with individuals with FASD across the life span. Blackburn (2010) reported families' concern that many professionals available to support their children were not knowledgeable about the condition. These included professionals within educational settings across the age range as well as those supporting short break services, and out-of- and after-school services.

One implication of this may be that children with FASD are not sufficiently well understood in early childhood settings. The following extract from Carel (2016: 249) highlights how bewildering an educational environment can be for children with FASD, and how difficult it might be for them to excel in education:

Let us reflect on the courage, fortitude and optimism required from such a child [with FASD] each morning as she gets ready for school. She knows the day will be confusing, that her experience of it will include gaps and sensory overload; she knows that others will treat her in a patronizing or impatient way, and that she will be told off for things that are beyond her control (for example, being loud when her impulse control is significantly impaired). She fears her own emotional lability, and is often frightened of what she may do and the consequences of her actions. She often does not remember or know what the day will bring, due to impaired memory (Is today Saturday? Do I have school today? What lessons are we having?). And yet, she will courageously – possibly more courageously than we can imagine – get herself ready to the best of her ability (one sock only, pyjama top still on) and set out to live another day in her bewildering, overwhelming, and often frightening reality.

This book aims to enable and empower early childhood professionals to support children with FASD to excel in their areas of interest and ability. The book further aims to address the paucity of knowledge and information about FASD in the early childhood workforce, and equip professionals to support children and families sensitively.

Conclusion

Early childhood professionals have an important role to play in supporting and scaffolding young children's learning and development. This chapter has highlighted the importance of early childhood inclusion and the paucity of knowledge amongst the early childhood workforce about the effects of prenatal exposure to alcohol. Knowledge and information will provide professionals with the opportunity to apply appropriate interventions for children and their families, and contribute to raising awareness and prevention of future risk. The next chapter will discuss the wide range of developmental delays and difficulties that fall under the umbrella term of FASD. Following this, further chapters will discuss policy, theory, pedagogy and support, and introduce a framework for knowledge and understanding as a tool to develop inclusive practice for young children prenatally exposed to alcohol.

Reflecting on your practice

- What kind of support might a child with FASD need in an early childhood setting?
- How and what tools would you use to assess a child whom you thought might have been prenatally exposed to alcohol?
- How do you think you need to approach your work with families for children with PEA/FASD?
- What other professionals do you think might be involved?

Notes

1 *DNA methylation* is an epigenetic mechanism that occurs by the addition of a methyl (CH_3) group to DNA, thereby often modifying the function of the genes.

2   Epigenetics is the study of heritable changes in gene expression (active versus inactive genes) that do not involve changes to the underlying DNA sequence.

3   Sure Start is a UK government programme which provides services for pre-school children and their families. It works to bring together early education, childcare, health and family support. Services provided include advice on health care and child development, play schemes, parenting classes, family outreach support, and adult education and advice.

Chapter 2

Fetal Alcohol Spectrum Disorders

Introduction

The purpose of this chapter is to provide a fuller explanation of Fetal Alcohol Spectrum Disorders (FASD), explain the range of effects that might result from prenatal exposure to alcohol (PEA) for children and families, discuss the different family structures in which children with FASD might live and grow up, and signpost early childhood professionals (ECPs) to a range of organisations that offer support and advice for families. In this publication the term FASD is used to include the full range of effects that arise from PEA. The aim is not to encourage ECPs to diagnose children or stigmatise families, but to support their knowledge and understanding about the complex and compounding factors in this area of early childhood inclusion and intervention.

Fetal Alcohol Spectrum Disorders

The term Fetal Alcohol Spectrum Disorders is used as an umbrella term and refers to a range of delays and difficulties associated with alcohol consumption in pregnancy. A large number of children are born every year in the UK with lifelong physical, behavioural or cognitive disabilities caused by alcohol consumption during pregnancy. The prevalence or occurrence of children born with FASD is not known in the UK, although estimates from international prevalence rates vary between 1% to 9%, depending on the country and socioeconomic and sociocultural variables (BMA, 2016: 7). FASD has a substantial impact on the lives of children and those who live with them, support them and educate them.

The adverse effects of PEA on the developing fetus and child lie within a continuum and represent a spectrum of structural anomalies, and behavioural and neurocognitive impairments. The range of child delays and difficulties associated with this vary in severity and outcomes, depending on the level, pattern and timing of maternal alcohol consumption. They also worsen over time as children mature and the demands on their cognition, sensory integration system, communicative competence, and self-regulation and control increase. This is especially the case when effective early childhood intervention and support have not been available to the child and their family/community.

Why is alcohol in pregnancy harmful?

Alcohol is a teratogenic compound that readily crosses the placenta, as described in the previous chapter. Because a fetus does not yet have a developed blood filtration system, the fetus is unprotected from alcohol circulating in the blood system. There are a number of ways PEA can affect the fetus, and these can result in a wide range of problems. The most severe effects are the intellectual disabilities associated with the adverse impact of alcohol on fetal brain development and the central nervous system (CNS). Damage to the brain is often, though not always, accompanied by distinctive facial anomalies, physical and emotional developmental problems, memory and attention deficits, and a variety of cognitive and behavioural problems. There is also the risk of children developing so called secondary disabilities such as mental health problems, and alcohol and drug addiction (BMA, 2016: 3).

What is the range of conditions that are included in FASD?

A range of delays, difficulties and disabilities are classified under the umbrella term FASD. This is a non-diagnostic term that covers several medical diagnoses, from the full presentation of fetal alcohol syndrome (FAS), to a set of conditions including partial fetal alcohol syndrome (PFAS), alcohol-related birth defects (ARBD) and alcohol-related neurodevelopmental disorders (ARND). PFAS, ARND and ARBD show some, but not all, of the features of FAS as shown in Table 2.1.

Children who are diagnosed with FAS – which is the most clinically recognisable form of FASD – exhibit the full range of effects of PEA, which is characterised by a pattern of anomalies including:

- *CNS dysfunction* – damage to the CNS results in the permanent impairment of brain function which may lead to intellectual and developmental disabilities, attention deficits, poor social understanding, hyperactivity, poor coordination and planning, poor muscle tone, verbal working memory deficits, receptive language deficits, executive functioning deficits (for example, difficulty in organising and planning), slower processing speed and the inability to learn from the consequences of their behaviour.
- *Facial anomalies* – FAS is commonly associated with unusual facial features including short palpebral fissures, a thin upper lip vermillion and a smooth philtrum pre- and postnatal.

Table 2.1 Diagnoses that fall under the umbrella term of Fetal Alcohol Spectrum Disorders

Educational or diagnostic term	Factors required for confirmation/diagnosis
Fetal alcohol syndrome (FAS)	Confirmed exposure to maternal alcohol; Facial dysmorphology; Growth retardation; and Central nervous system dysfunction
Partial FAS (PFAS)	Confirmed exposure to maternal alcohol; Facial dysmorphology; and either Growth retardation or Central nervous system dysfunction
Alcohol-related neurodevelopmental disorders (ARND)	Confirmed exposure to maternal alcohol; and Central nervous system dysfunction
Alcohol-related birth defects (ARBD)	Presence of congenital anomalies, e.g. cardiac, skeletal, renal, ocular, auditory – known to be associated with prenatal alcohol exposure

- *Growth deficiency* – babies born with FAS are commonly smaller than other babies and typically remain smaller throughout their lives (BMA, 2016: 3–6).

However, this does not mean that children with FAS are more severely affected than children with other diagnoses as within any diagnostic criteria the range of delays and difficulties experienced by children can be wide and varied.

Why do we need to recognise and diagnose FASD?

FASD is the leading non-genetic cause of disability in the Western world (British Medical Association, 2007). This means that unlike genetic conditions, it is entirely preventable. Although diagnosis is accompanied by a degree of stigma for children and their families, the argument for diagnosis can be made on the following grounds:

- Diagnosis is important for children and young people as it gives them identity and enables them to understand their own difficulties in daily life (Blackburn et al., 2012).
- Diagnosis of the primary condition helps to reduce the likelihood of secondary disabilities such as poor mental health.
- Diagnosis may lead to more accurately targeted and effective support as often children with FASD are either undiagnosed, or diagnosed with an alternative condition such as autism, attention deficit hyperactivity disorder (ADHD) or both of these (Blackburn et al., 2012). Whilst interventions targeted at alternative or co-existing conditions may be partially effective, if they do not work, educators will not have the neuroscientific understanding to adapt pedagogy based on a full and accurate diagnosis.
- Diagnosis may lead to improved community and societal understanding of the condition.
- Diagnosis helps to raise awareness about the risks of PEA. Clearly in the longer term, this has the potential to reduce the number of children born with FASD.

A number of authors describe the incidence of one birth of a child with FASD as community or societal failure, or a matter of social justice and inequality (Gray, 2013; Elliott, 2013; Karr-Morse-Wiley, 1997). This is because there are wider issues and concerns associated with FASD. These relate to the context in which it is acceptable and possible for women to drink alcohol in pregnancy, including price and availability of alcohol issues, but also because there are complex factors related to FASD. For example, in a study that was undertaken with aboriginal populations in Australia, Elliott (2013) recorded the following characteristics of children with FASD:

- 35% are born pre-term
- 65% are born with low birth weight
- only 7% are diagnosed at birth, the average age of diagnosis is 3.3 years
- 53% have microcephaly (small head circumference associated with an underdeveloped brain)
- 24% have significant birth defects
- 85% have behavioural problems
- 40% live with a birth parent (therefore 60% live with foster/adopted parents)
- 51% have a sibling with FASD.

Prematurity can be defined in terms of gestational age or birth weight. Each year in England, around 10,000 children are born very preterm (at less than 32 weeks' gestation) and a further 60,000 are born moderately preterm (at 32–36 weeks' gestation). The number of preterm births has increased in the last two decades, and more preterm children are surviving due to improved neonatal care (National Neonatal Audit Programme, 2015). However, the prevalence of cognitive, behavioural and emotional problems in preterm populations has not changed. In particular, children born preterm have been found to experience specific learning problems including difficulties with mathematics, visual-spatial skills, memory and attention. There is still much we do not know about the nature and spectrum of these learning difficulties, their long-term consequences, and how to deal with them. In particular, there is controversy about whether moderately preterm children experience similar but milder learning problems than children born very preterm. This is compounded by any difficulties associated with PEA. Children born with extremely low birth weight (ELBW) of less than 1,000 grams have been found to require some form of special educational support, and experience particular difficulty with either numeracy or reading (Bowen et al., 2002)

It is thought that up to 80% of children with FASD enter foster or adoption placement (Streissguth et al., 1985). Sometimes children with FASD experience multiple foster placements and can be difficult to place for adoption due to their challenging behaviour (Blackburn et al., 2012). This means that they may have difficulties developing and sustaining relationships with others. Elliott's findings also suggest that if there is already a child with FASD in the family, this should trigger more support for the family in future pregnancies.

Given the characteristics noted by Elliott (2013) and the arguments noted above, the imperative for diagnosis can be related to personal, psychological, educational and societal benefits. Sir Al Aynsley-Green puts it this way:

> Exposure to alcohol before birth is the most important preventable cause of brain damage in children today affecting substantial numbers of children. Its effects range from devastating physical and learning disabilities to subtle damage leading to poor behaviour, violence and predisposition to criminality. The human cost to affected infants and their families is huge let alone the economic impact and burden on our health, education and social care services and on the family and criminal justice systems.
>
> (Aynsley-Green, 2016: ix)

Currently in the UK, the overall rate of alcohol consumption in women is in decline. However, this trend disguises a more serious trend for very young women (aged 16 to 24) to drink at dangerous levels (to binge drink) (BMA, 2016). Binge drinking poses the most serious risk to the developing fetus due to an undeveloped blood filtration system, as mentioned earlier. Women who drink at dangerous levels are also more likely to participate in unplanned, unprotected sex which may result in pregnancy. If they continue to drink at their pre-pregnancy rates (which is not uncommon), the risk to the fetus is high. In addition, there are health and well-being consequences for women who drink heavily and/or engage in polysubstance abuse. These include:

- A lack of concentration, memory and attention;
- Mental health problems such as anxiety and depression;

- A risk of schizophrenia;
- Damage to the liver and other health problems;
- An overall weathering effect related to socioeconomic status, nutrition and living conditions;
- A risk of miscarriage and stillbirth.

It is worth pointing out that if miscarriage or premature birth occurs, the pregnancy has ended suddenly and prematurely and the mother most likely will not have been prepared for this. She may need support in coming to terms with either of these unknown and unforeseen circumstances.

Historically, information and advice to pregnant women and women planning their families has been inconsistent and misleading. However, guidance provided to women is now clear that the only safe level of alcohol in pregnancy is zero. This is because individual risk cannot be determined (BMA, 2016; May and Gossage, 2011).

ECPs are in an ideal position to identify, assess and support children's learning and development, support families and raise awareness. Their role in prevention and intervention is crucial and relies on their skill in developing relationships with children, families and other professionals such as health visitors and social workers. A further crucial skill lies in undertaking systematic and detailed observations of children at play.

What differences might I notice about children with FASD when I observe them at play?

Strengths

Children with FASD have many strengths and these should be used to identify opportunities for learning and development, and interventions for children. These include:

- Often gregarious, fun loving, caring and affectionate;
- Can be sensitive, loyal, kind and trusting in relationships;
- Can succeed in structured situations;
- Often enjoy repetitive work;
- Strong practical skills and tend be good at drama, art, woodwork;
- Strong sense of fairness;
- Strong visual memories;
- Good verbal fluency.

Difficulties

Some or all of the following may be observed in infants with FASD:

- Often trembling and difficult to soothe; may cry a lot;
- Weak sucking reflex;
- Little interest in food; feeding difficulties (feeding can take hours);
- Difficulties adjusting to solid food because of disinterest and poor appetite;
- Weak muscle tone;
- High susceptibility to illness;

- Unpredictable sleep patterns/cycles;
- High sensitivity to sights, sounds and touch;
- Failure to thrive (may continue to lose weight longer than normal after delivery);
- Delayed developmental milestones (for example, walking, talking);
- Problems with bonding (this may be exacerbated if the mother is also an excessive drinker and/or is depressed or finding bonding difficult herself);
- Small for age, underweight, may have been born prematurely.

Some or all of the following may be observed in pre-schoolers with FASD:

- Feeding and sleeping problems;
- Poor motor coordination, and poor fine and gross motor control;
- Short attention span, flitting from one activity/area to another, exhibiting butterfly-like movements;
- Demonstrates more interest in people than objects;
- Overly friendly and indiscriminate with relationships, may seek affection constantly;
- Expressive language may be delayed or children may be overly talkative (but lack richness of speech, thought or grammar complexity);
- Receptive language often delayed; even if children are talkative, they may not understand much of what is said to them; may follow other children's lead often;
- Inability to understand danger, often fearless;
- Low tolerance for frustration and prone to temper tantrums;
- Easily distracted or hyperactive (sometimes this is due to poor sensory integration);
- Difficulty with changes and transitions, prefer routines;
- Difficulty integrating sensory information, such as sound, touch, light, smells and movement.

Many of the above are demonstrated by young children in early childhood environments in abundance. However, when children exhibit these signs or red flags over sustained periods, they worsen (rather than being a transient phase), or they are more pronounced than experienced practitioners would expect to see in young children, additional vigilance and observations may be required.

How should I approach and support the family if I am concerned that a child may have FASD?

ECPs always strive to develop and maintain respectful, sensitive and professional relationships with families. The theoretical underpinning for working closely with families is discussed in the next chapter but is broadly related to a bio-psychosocial model (Bronfenbrenner, 1979). This acknowledges the significance of relationships within proximal contexts in which children grow and develop (such as the home and early childhood settings), as well as the relationships or linkages between them. This is especially important when there are potentially sensitive situations. Working with families is an essential and enjoyable aspect of early years practice. It was noted earlier that children affected by prenatal alcohol exposure often come to the attention of protective service agencies – they frequently enter foster care and may be placed for adoption (Astley et al., 2002; May et al., 2006). For children with FASD, therefore, the family structure may consist of foster or adoptive parents and family members as well as, or instead of, their biological family. Therefore sensitivity about relationship difficulties and family dynamics is required, particularly in relation to any attachment difficulties the child may be experiencing as a result of early life experiences (Catterick and Curran, 2014).

Birth families

If a child with FASD is living with their biological family, sensitivity and understanding about how parents may be feeling about the cause of their son's or daughter's disability is paramount. For the birth parents of a child with FASD, the experience of feeling guilty can be overwhelming and impact significantly on the relationship between mother and child. A birth mother (Whitehurst, 2010) describes this profound experience:

> I think all the time I was trying to find out if this was what was wrong. I was able to put a lot of my personal stuff aside because I was fighting so hard for him, but when you actually get that diagnosis it's like, 'Oh my, oh boy, what have I done?' ... It's very hard to forgive yourself when you've actually damaged someone's life irrevocably, you know. You can't turn the clock back ... I've said sorry to him so many times, and said I really, really wouldn't have wanted this life for you, and I really am so sorry ... but all I can do is be there for you to help you get through it, you know.
> (Whitehurst, 2010: 43)

In a study that involved a survey of 12 biological mothers' experiences of early support and advice (Blackburn, 2013), professional attitudes towards birth mothers included perceived hostility and value judgements from midwives, and mothers feeling let down by a complete absence of professional knowledge and understanding. Some mothers commented that this limited the possibility for them and other parents to make informed choices about their alcohol consumption during and after pregnancy, as well as their ability to receive appropriate support for themselves and their child following birth.

All mothers reported that none of their health professionals mentioned FASD. In five cases professionals knew that the mother was an alcoholic; one of these mothers was provided with an alcohol diary. In two of these cases, mothers were informed that drinking was harmful to their baby; however, one mother was informed that her drinking would not present a problem, but was advised not to smoke or eat particular foods (such as soft cheese or pâté). Four mothers out of the 12 were advised not to smoke and/or were informed of the detrimental effects of particular foods.

When asked directly about knowledge amongst professionals, mothers described professional knowledge as non-existent or unreliable. One mother commented that although her child was diagnosed at birth, she was not provided with information about her child's care and development needs, whilst other mothers reported that the paediatrician or breast-feeding nurse were aware of FASD, indicating that there are discrete pockets of knowledge. One mother reported that professionals had to seek advice about FASD from the internet. Parents highlighted the essential service provided by support groups in the absence of government and local authority provision, and the need for professionals to be aware of the link between mental ill health in adolescence and adulthood and FASD.

Despite mothers being aware that their child was developing differently from his or her peers between birth and the age of six, professional acknowledgement of mothers' concerns was not common. In relation to diagnosis, where professional knowledge existed and physical rather than neurological effects were evident, diagnosis occurred within a matter of hours. However, this was a minority of cases. In the absence of professional knowledge and overt signs diagnosis took from between one and nine years. The most common reason given for long delays or children not being diagnosed was 'no one is listening; even though I have told them I drank'. The ages at which children received a diagnosis ranged from birth to 20 years, with the majority taking place in middle-to-late childhood. In two cases, diagnosis is ongoing as 'no one is listening' seven years and 30 years, respectively, after parents raised FASD as a possibility. Two mothers commented that their child was diagnosed without their knowledge and they were informed a number of years later, or that FASD had been mentioned in the early stages by a health visitor or general practitioner (GP) but mothers did not understand the term and a diagnostic assessment was not forthcoming. One of the children in the study is currently being assessed by a number of professionals.

Even so, the issues for children who are not diagnosed, or not diagnosed early, are complex. Two young people now aged 23 do not want to go through the diagnostic process, believing it will achieve nothing. This is the very real issue of whether a diagnosis of FASD is truly a diagnosis or simply a label. One mother is in consultation with the professionals in the secure mental health unit where her child has been placed. The professionals believe his behaviour is attributable to his own drug addiction. Another mother is being shunted between professionals who attribute her child's behaviour to environmental issues (living in an alcoholic household). Of course, this situation will add to the problems the child faces and may make the diagnosis more difficult but it does not change the original cause. Mothers commented that their opinion is not valued by professionals responsible for referring their child for diagnostic assessment.

Case study (from anonymous parent, personal communication, 2010)

Rachel (not her real name) drank heavily and used marijuana throughout pregnancy. When her son David (not his real name) was born she was motivated to change her drug and alcohol habits. However, she found it difficult:

> When I was pregnant I couldn't get up in the morning without throwing up and having a drink and I knew that I shouldn't, but I couldn't function without a drink. I am impatient and I am fiery and he's also learned a lot of that. I did find it hard to be a single mum and when I did put the drink down when he was about six months, and the marijuana when he was about year, then I had a wake-up call, and then I had to decide just which one am I going to choose? My son or the drugs? Mentally I was unfit, I had suicidal thoughts, I had thoughts about harming my son, was seeing things, I was a mess, so having a baby and trying to deal with my head was difficult.

During his infancy period, therefore, David's experience of caregiving interactions and early relationships is best described as unpredictable and insensitive. In addition, he was sexually abused at the age of three by a young adolescent. Consequently, he now experiences difficulties in forming relationships with peers, engaging in learning, expressing his emotions, and physical contact with others.

When he started going to nursery, I knew he needed a lot of support, but I thought it might be my parenting skills. Social Services were involved then and I had to see a counsellor. I asked for CAHMS [Child and Adolescent Mental Health Services] to be involved when he was sexually abused, but that support only started this year. A nursery place was also provided for him. Speech and language therapy was involved when he was quite young.

David now attends a special school for children with social, emotional and behavioural difficulties, where he has the additional socio-emotional support necessary to promote engagement in learning and self-regulation. However, family life continues to be dominated by his hyperactive and inattentive behaviour and often aggressive outbursts as a result of damage to his CNS and difficult relationships. As stated by Rachel:

[We need] help to deal with the guilt, we are newly married and David has known my husband since he was about two or three, but now I think we're all going to need help getting used to living together. My husband can't sometimes tolerate my son's behaviour and then I'm stuck in the middle, and I find that difficult. We [David and I] are staying at my mum's at the moment while she's away, because my husband was totally ignoring my son. He [my husband] knows that his behaviour is not good; I think we just need support gelling as a family.

Educators can support birth parents by offering a non-judgemental, empathetic ear, and by recognising that the birth parent of a child with FASD will undoubtedly have experienced a degree of grief about their child's condition, and will be *living with the burden of the legacy this has left*' (Whitehurst, 2010: 52).

These accounts from birth mothers highlight the impact of guilt on relationships and daily life. The following (quite lengthy) account from the birth mother of an adult with FASD further emphasises the need for sensitive, empathetic professionals to work with families in a relational way:

Being the birth mother of two children with a[n] FASD is like living in a continuous state of grief, fear, confusion and remorse. I grieve at the loss of a normal life for my children. I'm afraid for their future and whether I will be able to manage my own life well enough to help them through theirs, and most destructive of all, I sometimes experience such consuming remorse, such crushing anguish that I really know no words for it.

My children were conceived to be individuals with hopes and dreams and the potential for good. I see in Seth's heart that he is a good person, someone who tries very hard at everything he does. Mick has always been the success story that parents of children with or without FASD are desperate to hear about. He will always be an example of the highest that people can achieve. He has come from being developmentally delayed as a young baby and child, and of course, the paediatrician's assessment that he could have been 'retarded', to having good friends, managing money, holding down a job and a successful relationship. He is an amazing person. Whether it was his own hard work, genetics or accident, I am grateful that Mick has grown up to be one of the most considerate, respectful and helpful people I have known. He is certainly a credit to himself.

Seth's future may not be so bright although I hesitate to make anything a *fait accompli*. At this time in his life his misfiring synapses and damaged neurons may have created a pathway with considerably more speed bumps which must be negotiated. I was reminded recently that my experience of FASD is not necessarily the experience of others. While I fear for Seth, there are many people with FASD who, like Mick, have achieved and will continue to do so who would prefer to see books written about the positive experiences of people with FASD than the negative. My experience with Seth has indeed been negative. While he was the most adorable child, he has become a very difficult man. I know he tries hard but when he becomes overwhelmed and frustrated he is often his own worst enemy and everything we try to do is ungratefully rebuffed. Mick, although prenatally exposed to alcohol, has only ever exhibited positive behaviour, compassion, solidarity and optimism.

Knowing Seth will have to live with pain, frustration and misunderstanding all his life touches me deeply. When you know that your child will need care and attention for quite possibly the remainder of his life, and will always need medication to keep him from killing himself or someone else, everything is a nightmare that hurts constantly. When things are bad, all I can do is hope that tomorrow will be better.

The very nature of the condition has forced me to closely examine my feelings and make a decision that negative emotions will not prevail over recovery, awareness and action. If they had, my children would have come in second to my addiction.

It was very tempting when I first made the discovery of FASD to pick up a drink. However, I thought of what my boys would think if the person they need the most in the world is the same person who is still abusing the substance that injured them.

I know at this stage they bear me no resentment, but that could easily change if I chose to drink, and although I wouldn't encourage it, I wouldn't expect anything else. I know of no other way to ensure my children have the chance of a happy and fulfilling life than to find an acceptance of what has happened and do what is best for them. If I can be the best I can be, my boys might have a chance to be the best they can be.

I was also tempted to pretend FASD didn't exist. I could have denied the condition as a way of coping, denied that Seth's symptoms were similar to FAS – I knew beyond a shadow of a doubt that I could have done it effectively. After all, if alcoholism is the only disease that tells you that you don't have a problem, then as an alcoholic I could easily tell myself that Seth didn't have FAS.

Thankfully that thought matured – if I was going to cope with this, I would do it on my own terms. I would acknowledge responsibility for his condition and contend with it that way or not at all. I would not deny it or rationalise it or attribute it to symptoms of ADHD, mental illness or drug psychosis. This was my doing and I would actively participate in Seth's rehabilitation as far as that might be possible.

To find courage and determination within oneself, one needs to experience an event that calls for those attributes, otherwise they may remain locked away, the individual never conceiving of the power that lies inside. When my children were born, I felt blessed and very very frightened. Never before had I allowed myself to be so completely exposed and defenceless. I knew that if anything untoward happened to my children, anything at all, then I would die.

But I did find strength and courage because something did happen to my children. If it had to happen this way, then I am grateful I was not denied the opportunity to discover this about myself. I believe that the depth of our grief is evidence of our love, and that while grief can be overwhelming and even unbearable, eventually it will come back to love – for our children, for others and for ourselves.

When I'm at my lowest I think that a mother could have done nothing that equals the harm I have caused and that perhaps they would be better off without me, but I have to remind myself of the many little things I do that help them, particularly Seth. If I were not here I wouldn't have the chance to make his life a little easier. No one would advocate for him as I do, no one would have the strength or the energy or the understanding or the love I have to make sure everything that can be done is done.

Adopted families

Families adopt for a variety of reasons, but in all cases the bond that unites adopted families bears both similarities and differences to biological families:

> Adoption begins with a process to parent a child not born or conceived of one's own body. Adoptive families are thus intentional families bound together by belief, will, practice and most of all love.
>
> (Rampage et al., 2003: 210)

The decision to adopt a child is not one that any parent will enter into lightly and can result from a number of factors, including:

- Infertility or the inability to carry a pregnancy to full term.
- The desire to provide a stable home environment for a relative (e.g. niece or nephew) when the child's parents are unavailable due to long-term illness (including drug or alcohol addiction or mental illness) or death.
- The desire to extend a family without the necessity for pregnancy.
- A religious or social desire to provide care for someone less fortunate.
- The desire for a single person or gay/lesbian couple to parent a child.

(Rampage et al., 2003: 212)

The process of adoption can be necessarily lengthy, complex and intrusive in order to ensure that suitable and appropriate home environments are provided for vulnerable children.

The challenges faced by all families in daily life are also faced by adoptive families. In addition to this, adoptive families face the additional challenge that every adopted child will have two families (the family with whom the child lives and the family they have left behind). The child may have memories about their birth parents and strong feelings of attachment towards them, impacting on the success of the adoptive placement and their relationship with adoptive parents and other adults. An increasing number of children are being adopted from abroad (Rampage et al., 2003), particularly from countries where there has been social upheaval or dire economic circumstances placing many children in orphanages and institutional care. This can increase challenges for establishing new relationships, and where the child may have a different ethnic or racial background to adoptive parents, the physical dissimilarity among family members means that the adoption will be more public and open to interpretation from others (Rampage et al., 2003: 211).

ECPs will need to be sensitive to the rights of parents and children for privacy about adoption, whilst at the same time encouraging families to be honest and open about children's birth history and any concerns they may have about the child's early experiences.

When children first join an early childhood setting, ECPs usually have a discussion with the family about the pregnancy, early experiences, and the child's likes, dislikes and preferences. This is a good time to discover any sensitive information and reflect on any additional concerns that might be raised.

Case study (from anonymous parent, personal communication, 2010)

Claire and Simon adopted Steven (not their real names) when he was seven months old. Steven was born at six months' gestation and his biological mother drank heavily throughout her pregnancy. He was diagnosed with FAS at birth and was cared for in hospital for the majority of his first seven months due to complex health and medical needs. Steven's difficulties include:

- Visual and hearing impairments;
- Heart problems (a leak on one of the valves);
- Feeding problems, difficulty over food choices;
- Skeletal problem (bones are not formed properly);
- Mobility difficulties which impact his ability to walk distances and run, small stature;
- He is doubly incontinent.

His biological parents were reported to be 'in denial' about their son's problems, claiming that any developmental delays/difficulties were genetically based and consequently they informed their wider family that their son had died. David's adoptive mother feels that being born prematurely decreased some of the later damage that would have been caused by PEA:

> I think Steven's a little bit different [from other children with FASD] because he has more medical problems than behavioural. He has got learning difficulties, but certainly behaviour is not an issue with him and I'm never quite sure whether that's because he missed the last trimester – he was born at 6 months gestation. So when I've been looking at other children who have gone full pregnancy, they've had many more behavioural problems than Steven has.

She also stressed the difference between biological parents and adoptive parents in terms of guilt in relation to PEA:

> I think the thing with having an adopted child with FAS is that I don't have the guilt thing about parental alcohol abuse, and we have changed Steven's name which I think is important. Every parent who has a child with a disability has a degree of guilt and what if scenarios, particularly mothers, wondering if they ate something or did something, and all the time the media pushes things on them to make them feel guilty.
>
> I've had people come up to me and say that we should put babies like that down at birth when I've been out with the children and people stare. I wonder how many birth parents have that all the time.

Steven now attends a school for children with complex and multiple learning difficulties. He is much smaller than his peers, who tend to baby him. He is often bullied by his peers; however, he is very popular with adults due to his friendly disposition. His early diagnosis and long-term stable home environment have been protective factors in reducing or ameliorating further risk of secondary complications.

If the child's family (whether biological or adoptive) knows that the child has been exposed to alcohol prenatally, then a referral to their GP would be advisable to determine whether there is a specialist geneticist or FASD paediatrician/psychiatrist available in the area in order to follow a diagnostic pathway. Diagnosis is complex and multi-faceted (Mukherjee, 2013) due to a number of factors. These include the reported lack of knowledge and awareness across a range of professional disciplines (Blackburn, 2013), different diagnostic tools and pathways, the number of different co-existing and overlapping disorders with FASD, similarities between the physical characteristics of FASD and other conditions (such as Noonans syndrome, Williams syndrome, Cornelia de Lange syndrome and others), information available about the child's prenatal and postnatal growth and development history, and the absence of any physical characteristics (such as obvious facial anomalies) for children who do not have FAS but other conditions on the spectrum.

Further to this, both biological and adoptive families can be signposted to a range of organisations, as shown below:

- NOFAS-UK (National Organisation on Fetal Alcohol Syndrome) (www.nofas-uk. org) promotes public awareness about the risks of alcohol consumption during pregnancy with the goal to reduce the number of babies being born with FASD. It further acts as a source of information to the general public, press, and to medical professionals.
- NOFAS-USA (National Organization on Fetal Alcohol Syndrome) (www.nofas.org) seeks to create a global community free of alcohol-exposed pregnancies and a society supportive of individuals already living with FASD.
- NOFAS Circle of Hope (www.nofas.org/circleofhope/) is a peer-mentoring programme which works to reduce the stigma birth mothers face by connecting them with other women who have had the same experience.
- FASD Trust (www.fasdtrust.co.uk) provides support for those affected by FASD and training/information for the professionals seeking to support them. It runs support groups for those affected by FASD across the UK, hosts various professional forums, and has a variety of training and other resources for those affected by or interested in FASD.
- FASD Scotland (www.fasdscotland.com) offers information, support and advice on FASD.
- FASD Clinic, Surrey and Borders NHS Foundation Trust (www.fasdclinic.com/ resources) has developed a resource page for families and professionals including a series of video blogs explaining aspects of FASD.
- European FASD Alliance (www.eufasd.org) was founded in 2011 to meet the need for European professionals and nongovernmental organisations concerned with FASD to share ideas and work together.
- FASD Network UK (www.fasdnetwork.org) is a social enterprise providing support to caregivers of children and adults with FASD. It also provides training for professionals and practitioners and advocates for services for people with FASD.

- UK and European Birth Mum Network – FASD (www.eurobmsn.org) is a network of women who consumed alcohol during pregnancy and may have a child or children with FASD. The network offers a place where mothers can share their experience and support each other.

Conclusion

Prenatal exposure to alcohol can influence children's learning, development and well-being over the life course. The most important time for recognising and diagnosing FASD is in early childhood to reduce the likelihood of secondary disabilities and relational problems in families. ECPs have an important role to play in supporting families by signposting to other services and providing information about healthy pregnancies. Families need sensitive, reflective practitioners who value and appreciate diverse family practices and relationships, whilst ensuring that children's rights to appropriate support and intervention are promoted. Regardless of the family structure, respectful and sensitive relationships will need to be established with families to promote the best outcomes for children.

Reflecting on your practice

- How would you raise awareness of FASD in an early childhood setting without stigmatising women/families?
- How would you encourage fathers to be involved in supporting mothers to ensure that their pregnancy is healthy?
- How would you work with a family sensitively if you suspected that a child had been exposed to alcohol or other drugs in pregnancy?
- Which agencies/professionals would you involve?
- What kind of support strategies do you think a child would need in an early years setting if they had been exposed to alcohol prenatally?
- How would you expect their learning and development to change over time?

Chapter 3

Policy for early childhood inclusion and intervention

Introduction

This chapter will present a brief introduction to the policy background to inclusion of young children with special educational needs and disabilities (SEND) in early childhood settings before discussing the argument for and role of early childhood intervention in developing inclusive practice for young children with Fetal Alcohol Spectrum Disorders (FASD) and their families.

Early childhood policy

Early childhood policy has been prioritised by successive governments from New Labour to the current Conservative Party. The provision of childcare and nursery education for under-fives and strengthening parental responsibility were prioritised by New Labour, in part so that more women could join the workforce, but also to ensure that all children had equal opportunities to succeed (Henricson, 2012). Early childhood was the period during which the foundations for future success and happiness were perceived by government to be laid:

> The early years of a child's life are critical to their future success and happiness. We are determined to invest in better opportunities for our youngest children ... we need to do more to provide help to parents with the difficult job of raising children successfully throughout their childhood and adolescence.
>
> (Home Office, 1998: 15–16)

Unfolding child and family policy developments have also interacted with wider social policy goals of tackling established problems with poverty and raising standards of educational outcomes for children (Baldock et al., 2013). With one in three children living in poverty (Baldock et al., 2013: 46) in 1988, New Labour was concerned about the risk that poverty posed to children and families, in the light of research evidence that had linked economic disadvantage to parental stress, low responsiveness in parent-child interactions, and a range of poor cognitive and social-emotional outcomes in young children. This included inadequate language acquisition, self-regulation, and confidence to interact or express their needs (Whitebread and Bingham, 2011). Consequently New Labour made an ambitious, and arguably naive, claim that the cycle of deprivation could be broken within two decades:

> [O]ur historic aim that ours is the first generation to end child poverty forever, and it will take a generation. It is a 20-year mission, but I believe it can be done.
>
> (Blair, 1999: 7)

The focus on poverty, disadvantage and troubled families continued through the Conservative-Liberal Democrat coalition government into the current Conservative term of office. This resulted in a range of new initiatives, including the introduction of funded childcare, children's centres, new legislative frameworks and an increased focus on children at risk of or identified with SEND. Although some of these services have contracted with austerity measures (such as the closure of children's centres), the focus on early childhood intervention to reduce or prevent risk/SEND remains.

Special educational needs and disability/early childhood inclusion policy

The UK SEND policy development has been influenced by international human rights agendas and the need to reduce the social cost of failing to provide sufficient support to children with SEND early enough to improve their future success and life chances.

Therefore, in line with the international agenda of the United Nations Convention on the Rights of the Child (UNCRC) (1989) and the children's rights and inclusion agenda of the Salamanca Statement on Special Educational Needs (UNESCO, 1994), New Labour produced the Green Paper *Excellence for All Children: Meeting Special Educational Needs* (DfEE, 1997), in order to link SEND policies in the UK with international policy trends. Following this, the *Special Educational Needs and Disability Act* (SENDA) (HMG, 2001) provided protection for children with SEND against discrimination, and the right to education in mainstream settings. The resulting *SEN Code of Practice* (CoP) (DfES, 2001) for education settings placed an emphasis on the role of early years practitioners to support families in identifying children's needs through observation and monitoring, and required settings to appoint a Special Educational Needs Coordinator (SENCO) with overall responsibility for children with SEND.

Further to this, *Together from the Start* (DfES and DOH, 2003) and the *Early Support Programme* (DfES, 2004a) focused on coordinated services for children under the age of three and their families through children's centres. The aim was:

- To promote effective early intervention services for meeting the needs of very young disabled children and their families;
- To identify and promote existing good examples of effective partnership working; and
- To support the strategic development of services for this population.

Full participation and equality of opportunity for children with disabilities was explicitly stated in line with New Labour's social cohesion agenda, as shown below:

> Effective early intervention and support can produce improvements in children's health, social and cognitive development and help tackle some of the many social and physical barriers families of disabled children face to full participation in society.
>
> (DfES, 2003: 4)

There was an emphasis upon the development of a 'helping relationship' and empowerment with the child and the family rather than from the perspective of an 'expert model' of intervention (Davis et al., 2002). Although originally focusing on children from birth to three years of age, this range was extended to five years of age in 2007–08. The aim was to help families and professionals move away from perceived crisis intervention (Carpenter, 2005) to planned, sustained intervention through coordinated multi-agency assessment and service delivery for children with disabilities from birth to three years old, and their families. Since there was an established link between poverty and SEND (Blackburn et al., 2010; Emerson and Hatton, 2005), this initiative would also seem to support wider goals of reducing the number of children living in poverty.

Removing Barriers to Achievement (DfES, 2004b) set the agenda for children with SEND within the Every Child Matters policy agenda, focusing on early childhood intervention (ECI) and professional training and monitoring of children's progress. Further to this, the *Childcare Act* (DfES, 2006) stipulated that local authorities (LAs) must ensure sufficient provision for children with SEND in order to comply with parental childcare needs. All of this signified an increased emphasis on ECI, particularly in early childhood, joined-up services and the need for early years practitioners to work with parents to identify children's SEND as early as possible, to improve their development and ensure social participation.

The landmark *Children and Families Act* (DfE et al., 2014) recommended a revised SEN CoP (DfE and DOH, 2015). The new CoP places emphasis on early childhood professionals (ECPs) working with parents and multi-agency colleagues to utilise outcomes from the developmental assessments in the Early Years Foundation Stage (EYFS) (DfE, 2014) to identify children's additional needs as early as possible. This is in order to provide effective ECI for children with SEND from birth to 25 years. Joint training and professional development for the various professionals dealing with children and young people with SEND has been highlighted in order to deliver a more focused emphasis on parental control over services available to them. In addition, local authorities must ensure that early childhood providers have sufficient expertise to identify children's SEND, as outlined below.

The Children and Families Act 2014 *(Part 3)* – *key points*

Definition of SEN: a child has a special educational need if they have a learning difficulty or disability that calls for special educational provision. A learning difficulty is a significantly greater difficulty in learning than the majority of children of the same age.

In this context, disability is a disability that prevents or hinders a child from taking advantage of the facilities generally available. Special educational provision is provision that is additional to or different from that which is normally available in mainstream settings. For a child under the age of two, special educational provision means provision of any kind. A child under school age has SEN if he or she is likely to have SEN when they reach school age, or would do so if special educational provisions were not made for them. The principles of the Act recognise the importance of the wishes, views and feelings of children, young people and their parents, and encourage ECPs to:

- Promote their participation in decision making;
- Recognise the importance of information and support; and
- Focus on the best possible outcomes for children and young people with SEND.

The Act:

- Requires a joint approach across education, health and social care to commission;
- Requires services and cooperation at a local level to meet children and young people's needs;
- Requires LAs to publicise these services as a local offer so that parents and young people are clear what support is available locally in terms of SEN and disability in the early years;
- Establishes a framework from birth to 25 years, with Education, Health and Care Plans replacing statements of SEN; and
- Sets out a new framework for SEN and a new SEN and Disability Code of Practice.

All early years providers must:

- Have regard to the SEN and Disability Code of Practice (discussed below). This means that they must take it into account whenever they make decisions about young children;
- Ensure that they have the necessary expertise to support children and families; and
- Cooperate with the LA in meeting its duties to children with SEN.

The type of support that children with SEND receive will vary. Two broad levels of support are legislated for:

- SEN support – given to a child in their pre-school or school. In pre-school, children under the age of five will be assessed at the age of two and again in the summer term of the first year of primary school. Reasonable adjustments will be made for disabled children.
- Education, Health and Care plans (EHC) – for children up to the age of 25 who need more support than is available through SEN support. They aim to provide more substantial support for children through a unified approach that integrates education, health care and social care needs.

The early years pupil premium is additional funding for early years settings to improve the education they provide for disadvantaged three and four year olds. Eligibility criteria are available here: www.foundationyears.org.uk/2015/02/early-years-pupil-premium-guidance-for-providers/.

Special Educational Needs and Disability Code of Practice: 0–25 years (2015) – key points

This is statutory guidance for organisations that work with and support children and young people with special educational needs and disabilities.

The leaders of early years settings, schools and colleges should establish and maintain a culture of high expectations that expects those working with children and young people with SEN or disabilities to include them in all the opportunities available to other children and young people so they can achieve well (DfE and DOH, 2015: para. 1.31)

The Code requires:

- Early identification and an early response to SEND;
- Identification of SEND with parents;
- A graduated approach to responding to SEND;
- A cycle of assess, plan, do, review; and
- The involvement of specialists where a child continues to make less than expected progress.

Four broad areas of special education needs give an overview of the range of needs that should be planned for, not to fit a child into a category:

- Communication and interaction;
- Cognition and learning;
- Social, emotional and mental health;
- Sensory and/or physical needs.

Children with FASD often have needs in all of these areas. For further discussion and reflection points, visit http://councilfordisabledchildren.org.uk/sites/default/files/field/attachemnt/early-years-toolkit-merged.pdf.

The Department for Education has developed a guide for ECPs to implement the revised SEND CoP: www.gov.uk/government/publications/send-guide-for-early-years-settings. ECPs are required to conduct a progress check on children attending their provision at the age of two in partnership with parents, in collaboration with health visitors, and taking account of the child's voice: www.foundationyears.org.uk/wp-content/uploads/2012/03/A-Know-How-Guide.pdf.

ECPs must also pay due regard to the Equality Act (2010).

The Equality Act 2010 – *key points*

Early years settings must promote equality of opportunity and must not discriminate against, harass or victimise disabled children. Settings must not discriminate:

- Directly;
- Indirectly;
- For a reason arising in consequence of a disability; or
- By failing to make a reasonable adjustment.

Settings must make reasonable adjustments to ensure that disabled children are not at a substantial disadvantage compared with their peers. This includes adjustments to any provision, criterion or practice, making physical alterations and providing auxiliary aids and services.

This duty is anticipatory: settings must look ahead and anticipate what disabled children might need and what adjustments might need to be made to prevent any disadvantage.

The guiding principles in relation to developing inclusive practice for all children are provided by the EYFS (DfE, 2014), which provides a framework that brings together two sets of requirements:

- The learning and development requirements;
- The safeguarding and welfare requirements.

These requirements have their legal basis in section 39(1) of the *Childcare Act 2006*, and apply to all early years providers.

The EYFS – key points

The EYFS is based on a set of guiding principles and seeks to provide equality of opportunity and anti-discriminatory practices, ensuring that every child is included and supported (DfE, 2014). The EYFS, in combination with the Healthy Child Programme:

- Sets out an inclusive approach designed to be responsive to individual needs;
- Requires settings to have arrangements in place to identify and support children with SEN or disabilities;
- Requires all providers to make information available to parents about how the setting supports disabled children and children with SEN;
- Requires practitioners to review children's progress and share a summary with parents;
- Requires all settings to promote the good health of children attending the setting, and to have and implement a policy, and procedures, for administering medicines;
- Expects all settings to appoint a SENCO;
- Focuses on delivering improved outcomes and closing the achievement gap between disadvantaged children and others.

This includes involving parents in identifying needs, deciding outcomes, planning provision and seeking expertise at whatever point it is needed. For more detailed information: www.foundationyears.org.uk/eyfs-statutory-framework and www.gov.uk/government/publications/early-years-foundation-stage-framework.

Working Together to Safeguard Children – key points

Early years providers have a duty under section 40 of the *Childcare Act 2006* to comply with the welfare requirements of the EYFS. Early years providers should ensure that:

- Staff complete safeguarding training which enables them to recognise signs of potential abuse and neglect; and
- They have a practitioner who is designated to take lead responsibility for safeguarding children within each early years setting and who should liaise with local statutory children's services agencies as appropriate. This lead should also complete child protection training.

Children with FASD are often at risk of adverse early experiences (trauma, abuse, neglect) and including them will mean working closely within interdisciplinary teams to identify, assess and monitor their progress. One outcome of the developmental check stipulated by EYFS (DfE, 2014) and/or safeguarding measures is that children might be referred for early childhood intervention services. For children who have been exposed prenatally to alcohol, it is important that the check takes account of any adverse early experiences such as being placed in care or attending multiple hospital appointments for medical and health needs. If the child has also been born prematurely then account needs to be taken of this in relation to developmental milestones and expectations.

Early childhood intervention

The United Nations has adopted two international human rights treaties which, when taken together, articulate the human right to early childhood intervention (ECI) for infants and young children with disabilities. These treaties, the UNCRC and the Convention on the Rights of Persons with Disabilities (CRPD), also describe the standards by which all states parties can guide the development of programmes, services and laws necessary to comply with the Conventions.

ECI focuses on children's early development and acknowledges the ever-widening population of very young vulnerable children. ECI specifically focuses on vulnerable children from conception until the age of six years, due to the rapid growth that takes place in children's early development the gains from ECI at this stage are unique and not evident in later stages of childhood. Infancy is a crucial developmental stage when an individual forms the core of conscience, develops the ability to trust and relate to others, and lays down the foundation for lifelong learning and thinking.

ECI can prevent risk factors from exerting negative influences on children's development. For children with intellectual disabilities, ECI can not only minimise intellectual delay, but other secondary complications as well. ECI programmes need to be designed on the understanding that all learning occurs in the context of healthy relationships between the infant or child and those who live with and love them. This extends to professionals working in early childhood settings who develop close relationships with children and families demonstrating observed dimensions of professional love.

ECI has the potential to alter the developmental trajectory and support familial relationships for vulnerable children, optimising individual potential and community quality. Successive governments' interest in early years has been demonstrated by a number of independent reviews related to ECI. The reports were related to health inequalities (Marmot, 2010), poverty (Field, 2010), parenting (Allen, 2011) and child protection (Munro, 2011), and had a shared aim of setting out government plans for further reform specifically and how those working with young children and their families could collaborate more effectively to provide support at the earliest opportunity to reduce the likelihood of poor outcomes through ECI.

Health inequality and ECI

In November 2008, Professor Sir Michael Marmot was asked by the secretary of state for health to conduct an independent review to propose the most effective evidence-based strategies for reducing health inequalities in England post-2010. Associations were made between a person's social status and life expectancy. Those living in disadvantaged areas had lower levels of education, fewer employment opportunities and poorer housing conditions, and were expected to experience more health problems and live shorter lives than those higher up the social gradient. Reducing inequalities in health was perceived to be a matter of fairness and social justice but would also result in economic benefits.

Health inequalities started in the womb, where the foundations for life-long health and well-being were laid. Because of this, the report called for a 'second revolution in the early years' (Marmot, 2010: 16), which would involve a significant spending commitment from central and local government to ensure that all parents had information about healthy pregnancies and child development, that children would have universal access to high-quality childcare and education, and targeted outreach support be provided to the most disadvantaged families.

Poverty and ECI

Frank Field's independent review on poverty and life chances was commissioned by the coalition prime minister in June 2010, and focused on the well-being of children (Field, 2010). The report included a strategic discussion about the nature and extent of poverty in the UK as well as how a child's home environment in the first five years influenced their ability to be ready for school. Of particular importance were a healthy pregnancy; good maternal mental health; secure bonding with the child; love and responsiveness of parents along with clear boundaries; as well as opportunities for a child's cognitive, language, social and emotional development. All of these factors influenced children's development, particularly for those from birth to three years old. The influence of the school environment did not compensate for poor experiences in the first five years, as Field (2010: 5) observes:

> By the age of three, a baby's brain is 80% formed and his or her experiences before then shape the way the brain has grown and developed. By school age, there are very wide variations in children's abilities and the evidence is clear that children from poorer backgrounds do worse cognitively and behaviourally than those from more affluent homes. Schools do not effectively close that gap; children who arrive in the bottom range of ability tend to stay there.

Access to good services was also important, such as health services, children's centres and high-quality childcare, but these were fragmented and not easily accessible to those who would benefit most from them (Field, 2010).

Parenting and ECI

In July 2010, Graham Allen (MP) was commissioned by the coalition prime minister to lead an independent review on ECI. Allen (2011) outlined the rationale of ECI programmes, with an emphasis on parenting behaviour, child development and outcomes, particularly during the first three years of life. He investigated the policies, strategies and programmes that 'helped to give children aged birth to three-years-old the social and emotional bedrock they needed to reach their full potential; and to those who help older children become the good parents of tomorrow' (Allen, 2011: xii).

The aims of EI in Allen's review appeared to relate to reducing social problems in society by reducing the number of children raised in homes where the caregiving environment was less than optimal. Poor caregiving presented a risk to children's social and emotional development, readiness for school, later outcomes, employment potential and future parenting capacity. In describing the benefits of ECI he noted that some of the largest economic returns 'had been seen in improving children's ability to communicate, something central to any child's social development' (Allen, 2011: 3). Although there was a central role for LAs in the provision of universal and targeted ECI, the formation of a national Early Intervention Foundation (EIF) was a recommendation from Allen (2011), later taken forward by the coalition government. The purpose was to provide a source of independent assessment, advice and advocacy on ECI with a view to 'breaking the inter-generational cycles of dysfunction ... resulting from social disruption, broken families and unmet human potential' (Allen, 2013: 2). This was to be achieved by LAs implementing those ECI programmes that were judged to be the most effective evidence-based programmes by the EIF.

Child protection and ECI

In June 2010, Professor Eileen Munro (2011) was commissioned by the secretary of state for education to investigate increasing concern about bureaucracy and lack of professional discretion within the child protection system. Using systems theory to examine how these unsatisfactory conditions had evolved, the review reinforced the emphasis on closer collaboration between agencies, the value of ECI, the duty of LAs to provide support and evidence-based services for children, bringing increased accountability for LAs and their statutory, voluntary and community partners for children's welfare.

The importance of early brain development especially during pregnancy and the first 18 months of life, resulting from nurturing environments, were noted. There was a recommendation for all early years settings to have a named lead child protection and safeguarding practitioner in line with increased safeguarding procedures within the new EYFS (DfE, 2014).

Generally ECI is understood to comprise a set of supports, services and experiences to prevent or minimise long-term difficulties as early as possible in early childhood (Dunst and Trivette, 1997; Guralnick, 1997). Those in receipt of such services are typically at risk for developmental, emotional, social, behavioural and school problems due to biological and/or environmental factors (Guralnick, 2004: 1). This is distinct from the broader term of early intervention (EI), which refers to intervention being used to support any child and his or her family as early as possible at *any time* in his or her education (European Agency for Development in Special Needs Education, 2005: 10). Infancy is a crucial developmental stage when an individual forms the core of conscience, develops the ability to trust and relate to others, and lays down the foundation for lifelong learning and thinking (Karr-Morse and Wiley, 1997: 12). Allen notes the importance of early brain development:

> The early years are far and away the greatest period of growth in the human brain. The connections or synapses in a baby's brain grow 20 fold from having 10 trillion at birth to 200 trillion at age three.
>
> (Allen, 2011: 6)

The current government has focused on perinatal mental health. In the 2016 Queen's Speech a Life Changes Strategy was announced to improve life chances for disadvantaged children with a focus on early intervention to reduce or prevent abuse, neglect and poor parenting in the early years.

In terms of prevention of FASD the crucial period of development during which ECI could be most powerful, i.e. pregnancy, is best viewed as a 'staging period for well-being and disease in later life' (Murphy Paul, 2010: 5). In some Asian cultures, a child is considered one year old at birth and the parent-child relationship to commence nine months earlier. As we understand more about the profound developmental processes occurring in the womb, conception, rather than birth, is increasingly perceived as the very beginning of child development. The womb is the first environment a child is exposed to, and despite the notion of the protective nature of the womb, there is significant risk potential for sensory, neurodevelopmental and organ damage from toxic stimuli. A more appropriate focus for intervention services might be 'fetal and early childhood intervention' (FECI) (including the early germinal and embryonic stages). With this focus ECI would then encompass both preventative and educational or therapeutic measures.

Intervention at any point in a child's life is recommended as worthwhile and effective. The emphasis in this chapter is on identification and support *in pregnancy and early childhood* in order to reduce or (where possible) prevent immediate risk, and improve development and outcomes in both the short and long term. Perceiving a developing fetus as a sentient being should be a fundamental principle of this objective.

Intervening early in childhood has the potential to prevent, ameliorate or reverse developmental problems in children thought to be at risk. The questions of how and when to intervene to achieve optimum effect, how to measure the effect, and who benefits from the intervention all need to be considered in the context of children's development.

As discussed in the previous chapter, children grow and develop within the context of multiple interacting levels of influence on the dynamics of their development (Bronfenbrenner, 1979). These influences interact with each other and the developing child in a transactional bi-directional manner. They also change over time as children develop and mature, and family dynamics and structure change. The harmonious interaction of these multiple layers of influence is crucial. If ECI services fail to work in harmony with families or policy agendas at the very least the consequence would be failure to achieve optimum outcomes. Theoretically, the child is at the centre of ecological models.

The greatest impact on children is found in the influence of family life and relationships[1] including factors such as maternal health during pregnancy, parenting capacity, family stressors (mental health, substance use, domestic stability/violence) and other family factors (size, structure, income, assets, housing). Other settings such as early childhood education and care settings are also important. All of the above factors can provide positive or negative influences on children's development. For example, 'good enough' or warm, sensitive, attuned parenting is a positive influence, whereas parental neglect and abuse place development at risk. Some factors present simultaneous protection and risk. The removal of an abusing husband protects mother and child but risks plunging them into poverty.

Other, more distal influences such as community activities, as well as local and national policies affect children and their families. The influence of culture, beliefs and attitudes to childhood, parenting and family functioning pervade all settings that children inhabit. In this regard, cultures that rely on the recall and verbal transmission of traditional stories (such as aboriginal cultures) are at increased risk due to the impairment of memory associated with FASD.

How and when to intervene

If FASD is not identified, diagnosed and supported with appropriate intervention *early in childhood*, secondary disabilities result (Carpenter, 2013; O'Malley, 2013), which encourage the development of a trans-generational process (O'Malley, 2013). Children with FASD become adults with FASD and raise children of their own. Karr-Morse and Wiley (1997: 69) note that women who themselves have FASD have difficulty using counselling due to their inability to link cause and effect or think ahead, making treatment for alcohol or drug addiction during pregnancy problematic. As noted earlier, pregnancy is a crucial period of child development.

Intervention can include universal primary preventative measures to reduce the likelihood of women drinking during pregnancy, health visiting and midwifery services to monitor the progress of pregnancy and fetal development, and provide crucial information to expectant mothers, as well as assessing maternal mental health and well-being. Secondary preventative measures may be targeted at specific, socioeconomic and sociocultural or other vulnerable groups. Tertiary measures might include therapy with mothers after their child's birth to support reduction in alcohol or poly-substance abuse addiction (smoking and other illicit drugs or over-the-counter medications are often used alongside alcohol), and to address the specific therapeutic and educational needs of individual children.

Currently in the UK there are few targeted interventions aimed at early prevention or intervention for prenatal exposure to alcohol, although there is now an All Party Parliamentary Group on FASD which aims to 'raise public awareness of the dangers of drinking during pregnancy; to support children damaged by alcohol during pregnancy; and to reduce the incidence of this tragically avoidable condition' (Bill Esterton, 2015, www.appg-fasd.org.uk).

The concerns over women's alcohol consumption and the high prevalence of children exposed to alcohol *in utero* have been mentioned in previous chapters. Around 79,000 babies under the age of one in England are living with a parent who is classified as a 'problematic' drinker ('hazardous' or 'harmful'), and around 26,000 babies under the age of one in England are living with a parent who would be classified as a 'dependent' drinker (Cuthbert et al., 2012: 30). Not all parents classified as problematic or harmful drinkers experience problems with parenting skills; neither is the author suggesting that all children with FASD are born into households where parents are hazardous, harmful or dependent drinkers, as many are not. However, it is noteworthy that a study of 268 serious child protection case reviews in England found that 22% involved parental alcohol misuse (Brandon, 2009, cited in Cuthbert et al., 2012: 32). The likelihood that some children with FASD will have experienced neglect and abuse during early childhood should be noted by those planning training for professionals and programmes for children and families.

Charities and ECI leaders in the UK have made policy calls for government both to maintain and improve ECI services for vulnerable babies (Cuthbert et al., 2012: 55), and to support children with special educational needs in emerging categories 'such as those born with substance abuse or alcohol addictions' (Carpenter, 2005: 176). Despite this, ECI is currently concentrated in discrete areas of professional or voluntary services, rather than being initiative driven or goal directed by government, and is rarely aimed at supporting the developing fetus.

These charities include the three major parent-led organisations in the UK, NOFAS-UK (www.nofas-uk.org), the FASD Trust (www.fasdtrust.co.uk) and FASD Network (www.fasdnetwork.org). These groups provide guidance and support for parents through local support groups, training opportunities for parents and professionals, and telephone support. The UK and European Birth Mum Network – FASD (www.eurobmsn.org), launched in

2010 from the UK, is a network of women who drank alcohol during pregnancy and may have children with FASD. The network is a place where mothers can share their experiences and support each other.

Similar organisations exist internationally, as highlighted in Chapter 2. The first FASD clinic in the UK, being led by Dr Raja Mukherjee (www.sabp.nhs.uk/services/specialist/ fetal-alcohol-spectrum-disorder-fasd-clinic), offers specialist advice on the behaviour management and diagnosis of FASD. The service aims to identify the disorder in childhood thus helping prevent secondary social and psychological conditions such as social exclusion and mental health illnesses developing in the long term. The service is available through the National Health Service (NHS) to any family with a referral from their general practitioner (GP) or other professional, or who alternatively pays for the service independently.

The Parents Under Pressure (PUP) programme is a 20-week home-delivery programme which works with parents receiving drug or alcohol treatment and who have a child under two in their full-time care. It is underpinned by an ecological model of child development and targets multiple dimensions of family functioning. Therapists work with parents to help them develop parenting skills and safe, caring relationships with their babies. They will report any signs of child abuse or neglect to children's services. The programme is currently being provided on a trial and evaluation basis to families in selected locations in the UK to determine its efficacy (Cuthbert et al., 2012: 7).

A study funded by the Glasgow Children's Hospital Charity is currently taking samples of meconium from hundreds of babies born at the Princess Royal Maternity Hospital in Glasgow to test for high levels of alcohol by-products. This will be accompanied by a maternal lifestyle questionnaire. Results to date suggest about 40% of mothers consume some alcohol while pregnant and that about 15% of women drink more than one or two small glasses of wine a week during pregnancy (www.bbc.co.uk/news/uk-scotla nd-36168729).

The 'Alcohol in Pregnancy – Training for Midwives Project' is an initiative of NOFAS-UK (2010), designed to provide useful positive health information about the consumption of alcohol in pregnancy to midwives who play an important role in ECI. This must surely represent the most positive aspect of ECI as 'maternity care is the earliest intervention of them all' (Lewis, 2007: 4). Further to this, Thameside Hospital Maternity Service in collaboration with the Hospital Alcohol Liaison Service, and Public Health, have launched the Maternal Alcohol Management Algorithm (MAMA) Pathway in their maternity unit. As part of this, using TWEAK (a five-item scale for harmful drinking in pregnancy), the questions below are addressed:

- Tolerance: how many drinks does it take to make you feel high?
- Worry: have close friends or relatives complained about your drinking in the past year?
- Eye opener: do you sometimes take a drink in the morning when you wake up?
- Amnesia: has a friend or family member ever told you about things you said or did whilst drinking that you could not remember?
- Kut down: do you sometimes feel the need to cut down on your drinking?

All women are now screened at their first appointment with the midwife using this tool. The screening is then repeated in the 16th week of pregnancy. Screening for harmful drinking will potentially improve pregnancy outcomes by targeting women for interventions to help reduce their alcohol intake during pregnancy. Postnatal follow-up will help prevent women resuming harmful habits, enhancing their ability to care for their new-born and preventing future alcohol-related damage to the unborn baby in subsequent pregnancies.

Women attending their appointment with the midwife will be given information around the potential risks of alcohol consumption during pregnancy as standard. This on its own can motivate women to change their habits as an awareness is raised of the potential long-term effects of alcohol in pregnancy. Those identified as being at higher risk will, with consent, be referred to the Enhanced Midwifery Service for more specialist support during pregnancy and onward referral into specialist alcohol services for support and treatment as appropriate.

One of the further benefits of the MAMA Pathway is that for the first time the results of maternal alcohol screening in pregnancy will be recorded in neonatal notes to enable any potential long-term impact of maternal alcohol consumption during pregnancy to be tracked and considered when seeking diagnosis of FASD in the child in the future. The information will also be shared with the health visitor to ensure ongoing support once the woman is discharged from maternity services (https://mancmidwife.wordpress.com/2016/05/10/mama -no-alcohol-no-risk/).

Early childhood intervention and inclusion for children with FASD is discussed later, in Chapter 6, where some suggestions are made for the structure and content of programmes in this area.

The challenges of delivering inclusion and intervention for children with FASD in terms of lack of policy focus have already been discussed. According to Robertson and Messenger (2010), the most significant challenges for the UK in delivering inclusive early childhood provision for children with disabilities more broadly have been:

- Maintaining effective communication with all parties involved;
- Developing a clear understanding of roles and responsibilities between professionals and families;
- Maintaining a high level of professional specialism;
- Developing trust between families and professionals and interprofessionally; and
- Empowering parents and families.

Currently qualifications for the early childhood workforce are undergoing change with the introduction of a new Early Years Teacher qualification (which includes a focus on child development from birth to five years) and Early Years Educator (National Vocational Qualification level 3). These are part of a government policy drive to improve quality for early childhood provision and reduce the number of children entering compulsory education at the age of five years who are identified with SEND (Blackburn, 2016; Blackburn and Aubrey, 2016). There are as yet no distinctive qualifications for professionals who work with young children with complex needs – for example, early childhood intervention degrees at either undergraduate or postgraduate level – although there are qualifications that include or focus on SEND to varying degrees, some of which relate to particular conditions such as autism. This is an area for future development, as a specific ECI qualification with a focus on interprofessional relationships, working and communicating with families, and specialist approaches to monitoring and assessment of children's progress has the potential to address the concerns raised above.

Conclusion

This chapter has provided an overview of early childhood inclusion policy in the UK as well as a discussion about the imperative for targeted early childhood intervention for prenatal exposure to alcohol to improve prevention and long-term developmental trajectories for children with FASD. The chapter has highlighted the high involvement of the charity sector to improve services for children and families and the paucity of policy initiatives in relation to FASD. The next chapter will discuss possible approaches to developing inclusive practice for children exposed prenatally to alcohol.

Reflecting on your practice

All providers need to know and understand the statutory framework and what it means for their responsibilities to children, staff, parents/carers and visitors.
   Consider:

- How do managers ensure that all staff are aware of their responsibilities to disabled children and children with SEN?
- How do managers know how well the setting is meeting its responsibilities to disabled children and children with SEN?
- How do managers ensure that they seek the views and hear the voice of the child?
- How are managers working with other agencies to address early childhood intervention for FASD?

Note

1 High numbers of children with FASD enter the social care system, resulting in children being placed in long-term foster care, multiple family placements or being adopted. Children with FASD, therefore, sometimes have two families – the family they are placed with and their birth family.

Chapter 4

Theory, assessment, pedagogy and support

Introduction

This chapter will discuss a bio-psychosocial approach to assessment and will then focus on the role of adults in supporting children with Fetal Alcohol Spectrum Disorders (FASD). It will also suggest some useful pedagogical and assessment approaches and interventions. This chapter is closely linked to Chapter 5, which provides a framework of knowledge and understanding for early childhood professionals (ECPs) and is aligned to the Early Years Foundation Stage (EYFS) (DfE, 2014).

The work of ECPs is underpinned by a set of guiding principles. These are that early childhood provision and services should be inclusive, relational, family-centred, strengths-based, ecological and reflective. Children enter early childhood settings with prior experiences, agency and competency. They are active participants in the contexts in which they grow and develop. The role of the adults and environments that support them needs to be understood within the context of a theoretical framework. The bio-psychosocial model acknowledges children's own genetic inheritance and the interaction between this and the multiple integrative contexts that children inhabit.

Bio-psychosocial theory

Bronfenbrenner's (1979, 1993) bio-psychosocial model acknowledges that children grow and develop in a social and cultural context influenced by the bi-directional interactions and relationships within and between the environments they inhabit. Their learning and development are therefore socially and culturally constructed through interactions and relationships with others in environments where meanings and languages are shared, as summarised by Bronfenbrenner (2001: 6965):

> Over the life course, human development takes place through processes of progressively more complex reciprocal interaction between an active, evolving bio-psychological human organism and the persons, objects, and symbols in its immediate external environments. To be effective the interactions must occur on a fairly regular basis over extended periods of time.

Bronfenbrenner (1979, 1993) described four interrelated components within his model:

- *The developmental process*, involving the fused and dynamic relation of the individual and the context.

- *The person*, with his or her individual repertoire of biological, cognitive, emotional and behavioural characteristics.
- *The context* of human development, conceptualised as the nested levels, or systems of the ecology of human development.
- *Time*, conceptualised as involving the multiple dimensions of temporality – for example, ontogenetic time, family time and historical time – constituting the chronosystem that moderates change across the life course.

Together these four components constitute a process-person-context-time (or PPCT) model that is useful for conceptualising the integrated developmental system. The personal activity, setting, caregiver and child characteristics are most likely to be most potent in affecting the course of development. They include those characteristics that either encourage or discourage children's engagement with features of their environments such as people, symbols and artefacts that:

> set in motion, sustain, and encourage processes of interaction between the [developing] person and two aspects of the proximal environment: first, the people present in the setting; and second, the physical and symbolic features of the setting that invite, permit, or inhibit engagement in sustained, progressively more complex interaction with an activity in the immediate environment.
>
> (Bronfenbrenner, 1993: 11)

The bio-psychosocial model acknowledges that development is influenced and shaped by biological, social, economic and ideological forces, such as family and other social relationships, and the influences on them from culture, society and policy as shown in Figure 4.1.

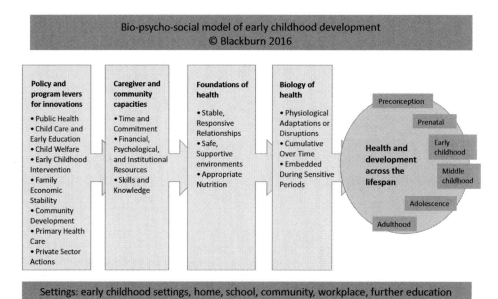

Figure 4.1 Bio-psychosocial model of early childhood development

Bronfenbrenner's (1979, 1993) vision was that its frame could transform the theory-application link between social policy and developmental research from a focus of 'what is' human development to 'what could be' human development when policy and developmental theory worked in harmony with them informing each other to improve children's developmental outcomes. This places a strong emphasis on the optimisation and enhancement of a child's life course, the production of positive and healthy development through the child's relations within the ecological developmental system. Development extends over time, beginning with the uterine environment of pregnancy and occurs within unique social and cultural experiential contexts as suggested by Bronfenbrenner's (1979, 1993) chronosystem and described as microtime. The broader macro sociocultural environment also influences infant development described as macrotime. For example, the rhythms and priorities of family life, practices and beliefs, the presence or absence of siblings, extended family and neighbourhood, parents' work, and government policy. The physical and social resources within the microsystem (the system considered to be the most influential on children's development) are especially important. This includes aspects such as the role and characteristics of adults and peers within the home and early childhood settings. The interaction or *relationship* between these environments is also regarded as influential (Bronfenbrenner, 1979, 1993; Dockrell and McShane, 1992).

New-born infants enter the extra-uterine environment with their unique genetic and biological heritage ready to shape their parents' behaviour, which in turn shapes the infant's behaviour in an interactive relationship between caregiver and child. Caregivers can also include ECPs, especially when children attend early childhood settings from infancy for a significant proportion of their time. This means that for children who are exposed to alcohol prenatally, the work of ECPs in supporting their postnatal growth and development has the potential to alter their developmental trajectory significantly through the development of effective pedagogy, support and development of inclusive practice. Assessment of a child's learning and development is most useful when it is contextually appropriate. Undertaking observations of children is best done when they are at play in their natural environments. In addition observation and any subsequent intervention should be undertaken in the multiple contexts in which children live and grow. For example, if they are attending a combined early childhood placement (a mainstream nursery and a specialist language centre) then assessment and intervention would naturally be equally undertaken and applied in both settings and where possible the home, and involve parents/families as part of the discussion. This would increase the level of consistency and predictably for the child and improve relationships between different contexts. The role and characteristics that adults bring to their work in supporting young children with FASD are discussed below.

The role of adults

The role and characteristics of adults within the microcontext of early childhood settings is a key aspect of early childhood inclusion and intervention for children with FASD. Of particular importance are communicative interactions, especially the sensitivity of professionals to children's social and emotional behaviour and their proclivity to interpret children's early signals and vocalisations, thus demonstrating mind-mindedness. This is especially true for infants, pre-verbal or non-verbal children, and children who are developmentally young for their chronological age. As children mature and grow, the role of adults is to support their emerging skills in the prime and specific areas of learning of the EYFS (DfE, 2014) with scaffolding, and respond to their growing interests with enthusiasm and responsiveness.

According to Vygotsky (1978) and Bruner (1983), adults mediate between the child and their environment, interpret children's early social behaviour and provide scaffolding. A degree of adult (or maternal) sensitivity to children's early social behaviour is needed. Maternal sensitivity is a central concept used in theories relating to attachment and bonding and early mother-child interactions, the most important tenet of which is that social and emotional development is contingent upon an infant developing a relationship with at least one primary caregiver.

This primary caregiver is usually, but not necessarily, a maternal figure. In this context, we are talking about early childhood professionals who work with very young children and those children who are developmentally young for their chronological age as is often the case with children who are prenatally exposed to alcohol.

Infants form attachments to any consistent caregiver who engages in sensitive and responsive transactional, bi-directional social interactions with them. According to Cassidy (1999), the quality of the social engagement is more influential than the amount of time spent in interaction. Ainsworth et al. (1978) defined caregiver sensitivity as the availability and alertness of the caregiver in well-timed responses to the child's signals, consistent with a degree of control and negotiation of conflicting goals. Sensitivity was conceived as individually constructed understanding and knowledge of the emotional signals between caregiver and child which result from 'dyadic construct' (Claussen and Crittenden, 2000: 116). Maternal sensitivity can therefore be observed as a behaviour pattern that pleases the child most, increases the child's well-being and reduces his or her distress. Observed dimensions of maternal behaviour in parent-child interactions have been categorised as degrees of sensitivity to infant signals, control over infant signals and unresponsiveness to infant signals (Crittenden, 1998). Each of these dimensions is also culturally influenced. Child characteristics might influence maternal sensitivity – for example, infants who are difficult to soothe or unresponsive to maternal dyadic interactions – and these are also culturally influenced.

Account is therefore taken of the individual characteristics of both children and caregivers, as well as the influence of the context of interactions, and the differential afforded by the same parent to different children at each age and stage of their development. Sensitivity in caregiver-child relationships exemplifies features that are manifest in early caregiver-child relationships and the influence of this on early communication development. For example, if children's early signals, whether intentional or not, were responded to in a manner that promoted motivation to interact with others, the foundations for social interaction, described as a precursor to language development, might be established. A feature of sensitivity for pre-verbal infants is the question of whether or not mothers treat their children as if they were 'intentional agents' (Meins and Fernyhough, 1999: 364) with a mind of their own and therefore communicated intentionality at the earliest stages of development.

If maternal ability to 'decode' the child's signals is a determiner of sensitivity, then maternal 'mind-mindedness' in interpreting pre-verbal infant signals and early utterances and behaviour would seem a feature of the healthy development of early skills, and this will now be discussed further.

Meins and Fernyhough (2006: 2) defined mind-mindedness as an individual's 'tendency to adopt the intentional stance (Dennett, 1987) in their interactions with and representations of others'. Mind-mindedness characterises social interaction involved in early caregiver-child interactions, and in particular, the proclivity of a mother to treat her child as an individual with a mind from an early age. Sensitive adults attribute intent to an infant's early vocalisations by interpreting the possible meaning of infant behaviour and vocalisations (Meins and Fernyhough, 2006). Therefore, in order to understand what an infant is trying to communicate in their early babbling and coos, it would seem necessary to recognise that the infant is actually *intending* to convey some message. In other words, when mothers listen and respond to their infant's early behaviours and vocalisations, they demonstrate mind-mindedness (Meins, 1997). They perceive these vocalisations as intentional communication rather than inconsequential utterances without agenda or meaning, and interpret them using past knowledge of the child and concurrent gestures (Meins and Fernyhough, 1999).

For example, in response to an infant's cries, a caregiver might say 'oh, are you a hungry boy?', based on previous understanding of infant behaviour, and consequently feed the child. In a study involving interviews with and interpretation of the infant vocabulary diaries of 33 mothers of infants between 11 and 20 months, Meins and Fernyhough (1999) found a link between infants' linguistic acquisitional style, maternal mind-mindedness and children's subsequent ability to develop 'theory of mind' or ability to understand others' minds. This is thought to be an important skill in social communication or pragmatic skills.

All of this stresses the importance of communicative interactions in early childhood settings and the significant contribution of relational pedagogy to early attachments. Attachment theory underpins the role of the key worker concept in early childhood settings stipulated in the EYFS (DfE, 2014).

Attachment and relational theory

There is a dance to childhood, a dance of reciprocal interactions that occurs between a child and his or her loving, supporting world as already alluded to. Caregivers shape infants' maturation through a meaningful system of communication, providing cues to guide interactions. The infant interprets the guiding hand and responds appropriately. The caregiver reads the infant's behaviour and takes the next step in a well-choreographed system of interaction.

The significance of these interactions and relationships to young children's development is emphasised in attachment theory, first proposed by Bowlby (1969) as a way of explaining the observed responses of young children and infants to separation from a primary adult. As already alluded to, children will develop a particular pattern of attachment to this primary adult (usually the mother) according to the adult's response to the infant's early overt and subtle communication signals (cries, responses to face-to-face interactions and language). Building on this (using a 'Strange Situation' experiment), Ainsworth et al. (1978),[1] and Main and Solomon (1986) identified different patterns/ styles of attachment, including:

- *Secure* attachment pattern
- *Insecure* attachment pattern, including:
  - Organised attachment patterns – avoidant pattern
  - Organised attachment patterns – resistant/ambivalent pattern
  - Disorganised attachment pattern.

These attachment patterns/styles are first evident between 9–12 months (Champion, 2010). In order to have a secure base from which to explore the world, be resilient to stress and have meaningful relationships with themselves and others, all infants need a primary adult who cares for them sensitively and who perceives, makes sense of and responds to their needs (Sargeant, 2010). This helps them to develop lasting relationships with others and to develop a *secure attachment pattern/style*.

Attachment difficulties can make it hard for children to:

- Gain the confidence and the self-motivation that comes from exploring the world from a safe base;
- Achieve developmental milestones;
- Reach their intellectual potential;
- Behave in a socially acceptable way;
- Think logically;
- Develop a conscience, have empathy;
- Become self-reliant;
- Cope with stress, frustration, fear, worry;
- Develop good relationships with peers and adults;
- Feel like a worthwhile person.

Insecurely attached children often feel, think and act much younger than their chronological age. Gaps in their development can create challenges for them in educational settings, where they are expected to behave with the same maturity as their securely attached peers. This can be frustrating for a child who may have the concentration and stimulation levels of a much younger child and may need learning tools, play activities, nurture, supervision, targets and boundaries appropriate to their developmental, rather than their chronological age.

This stresses the important role of the key person approach in early care and education. Building on this, Page and Elfer (2013) have developed the concept of an intellectual, loving, caring encounter conceptualised as professional love. This happens when caregivers can be self-aware, de-centre, emotionally invest in others and build a reciprocal and authentic relationship which enables children to feel valued. Blackburn (2015, 2016) found that the concept of professional love could be extended beyond the child to parents and wider family members, especially when relational approaches to inclusive practice and intervention were prioritised.

The concept of attachment patterns is not without critics and it is worth pointing out that there is a degree of cynicism about the ability of attachment patterns to predict children's long-term relationships or mental well-being from infancy to adulthood (Meins, 2016, personal communication). Nevertheless, attachment theory is useful as a basis for understanding children's early social relationships.

A parent/carer's ability to meet their infant's needs sensitively can be disrupted by a number of factors, including:

- Illness (mother and/or child), including postnatal depression;
- The birth of a child with a disability for whom parents are unprepared emotionally;
- Maternal drug/alcohol or other substance abuse;

- Premature birth;
- Frequent moves and placements in the case of a child who is fostered/adopted from birth (including multiple foster placements/adoptions);
- Removal of the child from the home environment for safeguarding or other purposes;
- Lack of response from the infant to the mother's care;
- Traumatic experiences.

This can result in the unavailability or unpredictability of a primary adult to meet an infant's needs, causing the infant to adopt an *insecure attachment pattern/style* (see above). This can have an impact on the way in which he/she forms later relationships and be particularly problematic if he/she moves into new homes (for fostering and adoption placements). Children with FASD may be exposed to one or more of these factors in their early years and can be particularly vulnerable to attachment difficulties as a result. Infants exposed to alcohol and drugs represent a prime example of how biological damage may interfere with the child's ability to fulfil their role in the interactive dance. Missteps at any point result in stumbles that damage the child's foundation for emotional and relational health. Alcohol has a direct impact on the structure and function of the developing fetal brain and affects the child's ability to make sense of parental cues; increasingly complex caregiving skills are needed in order to compensate (Chasnoff, 2010).

Children who experience attachment difficulties can communicate their emotions in a number of ways, some of which may be perceived by early childhood professionals as behavioural problems, often resulting in sanctions. Many approaches to managing behaviour suggested by professionals and introduced into early childhood settings are largely based on the work of behaviourists such as Skinner (1968). Such approaches are predicated on the assumption that children's behaviour can be controlled and modified via the reinforcement techniques of reward and sanction. For children with FASD, sanctions may increase underlying anxiety or communication difficulties resulting in pronounced patterns of difficult behaviour as noted by Chasnoff (2010).

By contrast, humanist approaches acknowledge the complexity of children's behaviour and focus on internal factors, rather than external control. They seek to address the complexities of social and emotional needs of children, particularly those who are high-risk. Davis (2003) highlights various studies that have shown how the quality of adult-child relationships shape classroom experiences and influence children's social and cognitive development. How ECPs respond to children's behaviour, in particular, can affect outcomes. For example, responsive, nurturing and attuned teachers are likely to diminish externalising or maladaptive behaviours (Tucker et al., 2002). By so doing, they are supporting children's social and self-control skills, sometimes referred to as pro-social skills. Communication and socio-emotional development are prime areas of learning in the EYFS (DfE, 2014) and these are areas of particular difficulty for children with FASD. Accordingly the focus of the pedagogical approaches suggested in this chapter relates to developing children's socio-emotional and communicative competence in order to improve relational skills. However, the next chapter will provide a framework of knowledge and understanding that relates to children's holistic development.

The role of and possible approaches for assessment are discussed below.

Assessment

It is important that assessment and intervention involve parents/families in a participatory and inclusive conversation and as far as possible take into account the child's natural routines, strengths, likes and dislikes.

Sensory preferences

Everyone has occasional sensory integration or processing challenges when the brain is overloaded by sensory information, or deprived of it, but some people go through daily life unable to process and integrate effectively the sensory information they receive through the senses of sight, sound, taste, touch, smell, body awareness and movement/balance. Children who are prenatally exposed to alcohol and/or have experienced adverse early experiences (including multiple foster placements or disrupted attachment experiences) may fall into this category as developmental trauma affects all areas of a child's functioning. They may get labelled as 'badly behaved'. This might be observed when children appear to be more inattentive or hyperactive than their chronological age suggests, as sometimes this is due to difficulties in sensory integration. Sensory processing disorder (SPD) relates to the inability to use information received through the senses in order to function smoothly in daily life. SPD is an umbrella term to cover a variety of neurological disabilities. Included in this are:

- *Sensory Modulation Problems* which pertain to how a child regulates his/her responses to sensations. This may result in a child being over-responsive (hypersensitive), under-responsive (hyposensitive) or sensory seeking, and some children may fluctuate between these positions.
- *Sensory Discrimination Difficulties* pertain to children who may have difficulty in distinguishing one sensation from another. We each have eight senses, including visual, auditory, olfactory, tactile, gustatory, proprioceptive, vestibular and introceptive. Each of these senses presents implications for the way we perceive and respond to our environment and perceive sensations such as pain, smell, taste, balance, sound.
- *Sensory-based Motor Problems* relate to children who may position their body in unusual ways and difficulty in conceiving of an action to do, planning how to organise and move their body, and carrying out the plan.

It is important to assess children's sensory preferences in order to plan and organise the physical and social resources within the environment in a way that promotes children's involvement in and enjoyment of learning. A sensory preferences profile is provided in Appendix A to this book to help with this.[2] Following completion of this, ECPs can actively implement strategies for children using the sensory passport (Appendix B) using the responses on the sensory preferences profile. It is hoped that the implementation of this profile and a sensory room on the setting will positively influence the development of inclusive practice towards children's sensory preferences.

When you have completed the sensory preferences profile (preferably in conversation with colleagues and parents), use the recommendations on the sensory passport to write personalised sensory passports for children and to develop your inclusive practice. The sensory passport provides strategies under the headings of 'sensory integration', 'communication' and 'transition and movement'.

Development Matters

Development Matters was produced by Early Education with support from the Department for Education. It is non-statutory guidance which supports all those working in early childhood education settings to implement the requirements of the Statutory Framework for the EYFS. Development Matters demonstrates how the four themes of the EYFS framework and the principles that inform them work together to support the development of babies, toddlers and young children within the context of the EYFS framework. The document also illustrates how the 'characteristics of effective learning' may be supported and extended by adults, as well as how they underpin the 'prime' and 'specific' areas of learning and development.

It can be used as part of daily observation, assessment and planning. It can also be used at points during the EYFS as a guide to making best-fit summative judgements, with parents and colleagues across agencies, in relation to whether a child is showing typical development, may be at risk of delay or is ahead for their age. The age/stage bands overlap because these are not fixed age boundaries but suggest a typical range of development. When using Development Matters, however, it is important to remember that babies, toddlers and young children develop at their own rates and in their own ways. The development statements and their order are not necessary steps for every child and should not be used as checklists: https://early-education.org.uk/development-matters.

Early Support materials

The Early Support Developmental Journals are designed to help families and early childhood professionals to better support development, especially where children or young people have special educational needs and disabilities. The journals are easy-to-use tools to help with observing, recording and celebrating progress, and to identify areas where extra help and support may be needed. All the journals aim to empower families and put them at the heart of decision making, supported by a coordinated keyworking approach: www.foundationyears.org.uk/2013/09/early-supports-school-year-journal/.

Engagement

Adopting an engagement approach to assessment enables professionals to reflect on their assumptions about children's active participation in activities and tasks, and adapt the learning environment to increase a child's interaction with it as suggested by Bronfenbrenner (1979). Using this approach, Blackburn (2010) found that some children with FASD in mainstream secondary schools were not engaged in learning for up to 60% of their school day.

Engagement materials were developed as a result of a multi-site international project that focused on learners who had co-existing complex learning difficulties and disabilities (Carpenter et al., 2011). The engagement profile and scale encourage child-centred reflection, supporting teachers to develop learning experiences and activities around students' strengths and interests. By breaking down 'engagement' into seven elements – awareness, curiosity, investigation, discovery, anticipation, persistence and initiation – the engagement profile and scale enable teachers actively to personalise activities for the child in a way which will invite their engagement. They allow them to explore questions in relation to aspects of engagement for individual children.

The Inquiry framework for learning is a tool that proposes pathways for inquiry into children's learning. It supports teachers to map the processes they go through in exploring and developing personalised learning pathways for students. It also gives teachers a means of demonstrating and justifying the lengthy but very valuable inquiry process which is an integral part of creating a student's personalised learning pathway: http://complexld.ssatrust.org.uk/project-information.html.

However, measuring child engagement alone may only demonstrate one dimension of relational aspects of learning. An adult engagement scale could be used in combination with the engagement profile mentioned here to measure those aspects identified earlier such as warmth, mind-mindedness, sensitivity, reciprocity and attunement. Furthermore, engagement is not a proxy for learning and development, and children's progress should always be measured against the EYFS and supporting materials such as the Early Support materials and Development Matters.

A commercially available resource to address adult and child involvement is the Sustained Shared Thinking and Emotional Well-being scale (SSTEW) (Siraj et al., 2015). The SSTEW aims to assess practice with a focus on both adult and child involvement related to well-being, self-regulation and focused thinking that is supported through sensitive interactions with others.

The Strengths and Difficulties Questionnaire

The Strengths and Difficulties Questionnaire (SDQ) is an assessment tool to measure daily coping ability for children and young people. The SDQ (www.sdqinfo.com) is a brief behavioural screening questionnaire for use with children and young people aged 4–17 years. It exists in several versions to meet the needs of researchers, clinicians and educationalists, and children and young people's strengths and difficulties are scored against the following components:

- Emotional symptoms
- Conduct problems
- Hyperactivity/inattention
- Peer relationship problems
- Pro-social behaviour.

The questionnaire can be answered by parents, educators (and other professionals) and children according to their chronological and developmental age. The results can be used to indicate strengths and difficulties in the above areas, and to inform future assessments. For example, if a child is thought to be displaying conduct problems, but both parent and educator SDQ completion indicates hyperactivity, this could highlight an overlooked aspect of the child's learning profile and lead to further assessment and specific interventions to address hyperactivity. One study indicated that children with FASD show needs in all of the above areas, with the highest scores being presented in those children involved in secondary education. Pro-social behaviour can be a strength for children with FASD, highlighting their very friendly nature (Blackburn, 2010). Carmichael Olson and Burgess (1997) also found that *young* children with FASD in particular are socially engaging, interested in others, very talkative and affectionate.

Returning to the bio-psychosocial model, it is important to remember that assessment, monitoring and intervention need to take account of the multiple environments or contexts in which children learn and develop, and that communication between adults (parents, professionals, para-professionals and wider community members) is supportive and effective.

Pedagogical approaches

Chasnoff (2010: 128–129) proposes six broad steps that parents and educators can take to support children's pro-social skills.

1   Provide opportunities for the child to have focused attention within conversations. Allow the child to be heard and to hear others sharing news from home and other social situations.
2   Be clear and consistent on rules and guidelines for ethical behaviour. Let the child participate in making rules about respectful interactions in the setting among peers.
3   Model social situations and practice interpersonal problem-solving skills that can provide positive ways for the child to assert her needs, resolve conflict and make friends. Ask the child to consider goals and reflect on options and their consequences:

>   'If someone calls you a name, what can you do?' 'If you do that, what is likely to happen?'
>   'If you need something and someone is using it for a long time and won't let you use it, what can you do?' 'If you do that, what is likely to happen?'
>   'If someone pushes you in line…'
>   'If you want someone to play with you and you are afraid to ask.'
>   'If someone makes you very angry (or very happy).'
>   Social stories may be very useful here.

4   Model respect, friendliness, firmness of purpose through interactions with the child.

>   Show the child what you expect.
>   Use affirming and encouraging language.
>   Stress the deed not the doer.
>   Notice and comment on what the child does 'right'.
>   Redirect behaviour using a firm, kind manner.
>   Say what you mean, mean what you say.

5   Provide opportunities to participate in group family activities and to learn to work together.

>   Divide and share tasks.
>   Plan cooperative projects.
>   Organise group games for fun not competition.
>   Assign developmentally appropriate jobs/tasks.

6   Provide opportunities for the child to learn constructive ways to handle controversy and differences.

> Have circle time discussions of current events.
> Suggest different 'right' solutions of the same problems.
> Hold circle time discussions to solve problems.
> Teach the value of diversity and acceptance.

Underpinning the above approaches are general requirements for children to manage their own behaviour. These relate to the need for:

- *Structure*: a stable environment in which children know what is expected and how to go about doing it.
- *Predictability*: a home and classroom in which children know what their day will look like and how their families and teachers will respond to them.
- *Consistency*: an environment in which responses to children are the same every day.

Effective communication and relationships between the proximal contexts of home and early care and education settings underpin all of the above.

Emotion coaching

Another emerging approach to supporting children's socio-emotional development and self-regulation is emotion coaching. Emotion coaching is a relational and skills-based approach to supporting children's emotional competency and self-regulation, and is more likely to result in decreased frustration and increased emotional well-being for children. This approach recognises that socially competent children who are able to understand and regulate their emotions are better equipped to go on to achieve higher academic success than those who lack impulse control or have poor social skills (Webster-Stratton, 2004; Graziano et al., 2007; Linnenbrink-Garcia and Pekrun, 2011).

Emotion coaching is based on the work of Gottman, Katz and colleagues (Gottman et al., 1996) and essentially comprises two key elements: empathy and guidance. These two elements express themselves through various processes that adults undertake whenever 'emotional moments' occur. Emotional empathy involves recognising, labelling and validating a child's emotions, regardless of the behaviour, in order to promote self-awareness and understanding of emotions. Such acceptance by the adult of the child's internal emotional state creates a context of responsiveness and security, and helps the child to engage with more reasonable solutions. The circumstances might also require setting limits on appropriate behaviour (such as stating clearly what is acceptable behaviour) and possible consequential action (such as implementing behaviour management procedures), but key to this process is guidance: engagement with the child in problem solving in order to support the child's ability to learn to self-regulate – the child and adult work together to seek alternative courses of action to help manage emotions and prevent future transgressions. This process is adaptable and responsive to the developmental capabilities of the child, with the adult scaffolding pro-social solutions and differentiating where necessary. By enabling children to tune in more explicitly to their emotions and problem-solve solutions that will help them to manage such feelings, and the behavioural consequences of those feelings, the child is engaged in proactively enhancing social and emotional competences. It also supports the child's development of 'meta-emotion', which refers to the 'organised set of feelings and cognitions about one's own emotions and the emotions of others' (Gottman et al., 1997: 7). Thus, emotion coaching helps to instil the tools that will aid children's ability to self-regulate their emotions and behaviour (Shortt et al., 2010).

This approach is supported by evidence that shows how thinking and reasoning and emotional processing are fundamentally integrated in the brain at multiple levels (Goswami, 2011; Immordino-Yang and Damasio, 2007). Our emotions and relationships influence our motivation and give meaning to our knowledge formation (Freiler, 2008). Weare and Gray's (2003) comprehensive review has also identified that interventions which teach social and emotional competencies can help to reduce behaviour problems. Indeed, 'emergence of behaviour problems has been linked to poor emotional competence in children, specifically problems in understanding and regulating emotions' (Havighurst et al., 2013: 248). More information is available from www.emotioncoaching.co.uk and www.emotioncoachinguk.com.

Social stories

Social stories are used to help teach social skills to people with social communication difficulties. They involve short descriptions of a particular situation, event or activity, which include specific information about what to expect in that situation and why.

They are simple visual representations of the different levels of communication in a conversation. For example, they could show:

- The things that are actually said in a conversation;
- How people might be feeling; or
- What people's intentions might be.

Comic strip conversations use symbols, stick figure drawings and colour. By seeing the different elements of a conversation presented visually, some of the more abstract aspects of social communication (such as recognising the feelings of others) are made more 'concrete' and are therefore easier to understand. Stories such as this, when designed with the child and rehearsed often, can help children with FASD understand complex social relationships.

Adult scaffolding and support

The central role of adults in children's learning was emphasised in Bruner's (1983) work. Bruner took the position that the adult had a central role to play in 'scaffolding' children's learning. Scaffolding involves the gradual withdrawal of adult control and support as a function of children's increasing mastery of a given task or skill. Adults must therefore engage the interest of the child, simplify the language they use, model processes or procedures involved in learning, such as vocabulary and grammar, and withdraw support when, through careful observation and monitoring, they are sure the child can proceed independently.

The concept of pedagogy as providing scaffolding for learning has been important for informing instruction in early childhood settings (Siraj-Blatchford et al., 2002). The crucial aspect is that the assistance, where it is required, must be appropriate to the needs of the learner. The pedagogical framing that professionals provide in relation to the organisation of staff, activities and grouping of children interacts with the instructional strategies they provide as well as the balance between opportunities for adult-led and child-initiated activities. In a longitudinal study that gathered evidence from a range of sources in order to investigate the most effective pedagogy in early childhood settings, Siraj-Blatchford et al. (2002) found that giving young children free choice to play in a learning environment that allows sufficient opportunity for effective adult intervention provided optimum promotion of a range of developmental outcomes including language and peer social interaction. This means that effective practitioners extend and build on child-initiated interactions and plan for frequent episodes of joint attention with individual children, as well as opportunities for children to participate in group work that involves high-quality content. Effective joint-attention episodes involve practitioners asking open-ended questions that promote children's participation and involvement in activities as well as thinking skills or cognition. Involving parents in children's learning and building on learning in early childhood settings are also important. Siraj-Blatchford et al. (2002) concluded that effective pedagogy included:

- Parents and professionals working together;
- A balance of activities planned by adults and those the children initiated themselves;
- Adults building on unexpected and unforeseen opportunities for children's learning that arose from everyday events and routines;
- Professionals making systematic observations and assessments of each child in order to be able to respond appropriately to their learning needs.

This emphasises the role of the key person in early childhood settings in developing relationships with children and their families. The dimensions of caregiving for developing warm, sensitive, attuned relationships with young children have already been mentioned in this book.

Interdisciplinary practice

Blackburn (2010) identified a range of professionals who supported the education workforce in assessing and monitoring children with FASD, as shown in Table 4.1. It is important that early childhood professionals are familiar with the wide range of professionals with whom they may come into contact.

There are many advantages for children, families and professionals of a broad range of professionals working collaboratively together in an interdisciplinary team. Interdisciplinary

Table 4.1 Range of professionals who might support children with FASD

Social worker	Speech and language therapist	Physiotherapist
Paediatrician	Occupational therapist	Educational psychologist
Mental health team	Dietician	Orthopaedic spinal specialist
FASD specialist	Geneticist	GP
Learning disabilities team	Inclusion support team	Psychologist
Play therapist	Music therapist	Orthotics
Children's charities (e.g. NSPCC, Barnardo's)	Police officers	Psychiatrist

teams are designed to facilitate professionals working together and learning from each other. Working in such teams also increases individual therapists' knowledge of other disciplines and builds a broader understanding of child development.

Interdisciplinary practice works most effectively when there is a partnership with families with an interest in parents' well-being and parents' goals in terms of their relationship with their child in line with the bio-psychosocial model (Bronfenbrenner, 1993). This means observing development of the whole child and ensuring that all aspects of the child's development are progressing well. Professionals work effectively in this model when they learn with and from each other in that each professional examines children's development and family processes from their own distinctive professional perspective. This perspective is respected by other professionals within the team that supports the child. However, each distinctive perspective forms one part of the whole perspective and the overall perspective is both holistic and consistent (Blackburn, 2015, 2016).

Conclusion

This chapter has discussed relational theory that underpins assessment, support and pedagogy in developing inclusive practice for supporting children with FASD. The chapter has introduced the bio-psychosocial model and suggested that this model is useful when considering the contextual nature of observation, assessment, developing inclusive practice and the application of interventions. The concepts of attachment, mind-mindedness, relational pedagogy, professional love and scaffolding have also been discussed, as well as interdisciplinary practice. The chapter has suggested some broad pedagogical approaches and possible assessment. The next chapter will introduce a more detailed pedagogical framework of knowledge and understanding in developing inclusive practice for young children prenatally exposed to alcohol/with FASD in early childhood settings.

Reflecting on your practice

- What observation tools have you successfully used for children with diverse and complex disabilities previously and how can they be adapted or modified for children with FASD?
- How will you assess and support the needs of families?
- Take time now to review the framework of understanding and knowledge in the next chapter to consider your current understanding and identify areas where you would like to learn more.

Notes

1 The strange situation was designed to assess how well an infant uses the caregiver as a secure base for exploration, and is comforted by the caregiver after a mildly stressful experience such as the mother leaving and reuniting with their infant. Infants are judged to have a 'secure' attachment if they explore the Strange Situation room and act in a friendly way before the separation from the caregiver, show mild wariness to a stranger during the separation, and are comforted and do not show anger when reunited with the caregiver (Rogoff, 2003).

2 The sensory preferences profile and the accompanying sensory passport have been adapted from a sensory preferences checklist, and recommendations and considerations from SsPIRE

documents that were developed by Birmingham City University and Studio III, working with the Wellcome Trust Birmingham Children's Hospital. They were developed to work with people who present with behaviours of concern. From this work it was believed that a focus on sensory experiences could help with the ability to cope and reduce behaviours of concern. The questions evolved from all the knowledge and experience of the team on autistic spectrum disorder sensory processes and of the ward in which it was trialled.

Chapter 5

Framework of knowledge and understanding to support young children prenatally exposed to alcohol/diagnosed with FASD

This framework has been developed to provide knowledge and understanding for early childhood professionals (ECPs) to support children who are prenatally exposed to alcohol. Some of these children will have a diagnosis of Fetal Alcohol Spectrum Disorders (FASD); however, many will not. The framework is aligned with the themes of the Early Years Foundation Stage (EYFS) (DfE, 2014), in order to increase its usefulness to ECPs.

The EYFS is underpinned by an ethos that children are born ready, able and eager to learn. They actively reach out to interact with other people, and in the world around them. Development is not an automatic process, however. It depends on each unique child having opportunities to interact in positive relationships and enabling environments. The concepts of relational pedagogy and professional love in developing inclusive practice have been discussed in this book and are seen as central to interdisciplinary practice in the assessment, monitoring and support for children with FASD and their families. This framework hereafter uses the term FASD to include those children who are prenatally exposed to alcohol and not diagnosed with FASD as well as those who are, for the purposes of simplicity, and is organised under the following EYFS themes:

1   A unique child: how to understand and address each child's strengths and needs.
2   Positive relationships: with staff, parents/carers, other agencies and peers.
3   Enabling environments: how to create good indoor and outdoor environments for children with FASD.
4   Learning and development: priorities in development, adjustments that can be made to activities.

Each area is linked to resources which professionals might use to deepen their knowledge and skills in this area. These resources include published papers, audio-visual material, and a range of reports and guidelines related to the competency's topic.

I A unique child

Number	Competency
1	You understand that the term FASD is a broad umbrella term for a range of delays and difficulties resulting from prenatal exposure to alcohol. You have read some basic information and understand the broad range of delays and difficulties that children might experience. You know where to look for further information, for example: www.cdc.gov/ncbddd/fasd/facts.html.
2	You understand that children exposed to alcohol prenatally may not live with their biological parents as high numbers of children with FASD enter the social care system. They may have two families (the one they live with and a biological family). They may have experienced multiple family placements (and/or adverse early experiences), and as a result communicate and express themselves in unusual and unpredictable ways. You have developed a range of strategies to support children with FASD in this area such as circle time discussions and social stories about diverse family structures and practices. You know how to access your Early Help resources within your local authority. A tool to record children's home and family experiences can be found here: www.pac-uk.org/wp-content/uploads/2016/04/Me-And-My-World.pdf. Support for children affected by adoption and permanency can be found here: www.pac-uk.org.
3	You understand the way in which prenatal exposure to alcohol influences differences in development and you know how this impacts how the child learns. You can assess and identify the key strengths, interests and challenges of children with FASD. Find out more at: www.rise.duke.edu/download/FASD_Guide.pdf and www.gov.mb.ca/healthychild/fasd/fasdeducators_en.pdf. See also this *British Journal of Special Education* article: http://onlinelibrary.wiley.com/doi/10.1111/j.1467-8578.2010.00471.x/abstract.
4	You know that children who are prenatally exposed to alcohol may experience problems with social, emotional and mental health. You know how to access your local Children and Adolescent Mental Health Services www.nhs.uk/NHSEngland/AboutNHSservices/mental-health-services-explained/Pages/about-childrens-mental-health-services.aspx. You observe, assess and monitor children for signs of mental health problems. You include a range of strategies to promote positive social, emotional and mental health such as nurture groups, circle time activities and positive behaviour management policies.
5	You understand that children prenatally exposed to alcohol are at risk from premature birth and that this can increase risk factors for delays and difficulties for children as well as parent-child relationships. You know where to find out more and refer parents for help, for example: www.bliss.org.uk.
6	You understand that using the child's interests and favourite activities is very important in gaining and maintaining their attention, and you build in many opportunities for the child to engage with these.
7	You understand the need to elicit much of your information on the child before they start, from their parents/carers, and finding out about the child's prenatal history and early experiences. You also endeavour to find out about the child's interests, skills, dislikes, fears, means of communication, medical and safety needs, and ways to comfort them, before they start.
8	You observe and assess each child across a variety of situations and learn to monitor and interpret their pre-verbal and non-verbal signals to understand their response to situations and ascertain their physical and socio-emotional well-being. You are familiar with a range of observation tools (mentioned in Chapter 4).

Number	Competency
9	You spend time observing, assessing and supporting children's speech, language and communication, and provide reasons and opportunities to communicate within your setting. You know how to access advice from a speech and language therapist, how to refer children and how to implement any strategies/targets they might suggest for children with FASD. Find out more: www.chimat.org.uk/beststart/speech.
10	You know that some children with FASD may find physical contact difficult and know to use this sensitively when playing and working with children.
11	You are able to assess a child's sensory needs and have strategies to help address these (see separate sensory profile and considerations in the appendices). Find out more: www.fasdoutreach.ca/elearning.
12	You understand that children with FASD often find social interaction difficult. You observe and assess the child's social preferences and ability, and take steps to help the child to play and work with others.
13	You ensure that the perspective of the child is taken when making decisions on how to engage and work with him/her. You understand that a child's actions need to be understood in terms of how their FASD might influence these and adjust your response accordingly. You understand that behaviour is a means of communication especially for young children who have difficulty expressing their emotions, and you adjust your responses to unwanted behaviour accordingly.
14	You know that children with FASD may have been diagnosed with other conditions too (attention deficit hyperactivity disorder (ADHD), speech, language and communication difficulties, attachment difficulties).
15	You create a profile of each child, setting out key information (for example, their likes, dislikes, interests, fears and forms of communication), based on close observation and information given by the child's parents/carers, and you use this to inform plans and practice.
16	You understand the need and plan for a transdisciplinary assessment of children on a regular basis and at key transition times such as the transition from an early childhood setting to primary school.
17	You understand that children with FASD may need nutritional supplements due to restrictions in food choices, feeding difficulties or digestive problems. You know where to find support with this: www.nutrition.org.uk/nutritionscience/life/880-preschoolchildren.html and www.firststepsnutrition.org/index.html.

I sometimes think of him like a changeling, a very nice, very beautiful changeling but someone who is also like a jigsaw, so many different pieces and nobody seems to have the time to put the picture together and see the whole child!

(Parent of a child with an FASD, Carpenter et al., 2013: xxiv)

2 Positive relationships

Number	Competency
1	You welcome parents and carers, value their knowledge and listen to their concerns. You have a means of finding out what each parent would like to work on, what their child enjoys at home and how best to comfort the child when distressed. You have a number of different ways of involving and informing parents/carers (for example, discussing goals, reports, training, email, DVD, photos, parent helpline). You know that positive relationships are a key factor in building resilience and positive mental well-being for children and families. Find out more: www.chimat.org.uk/ beststart/relationships.
2	You know that some children who have been exposed prenatally to alcohol will not have been diagnosed with FASD and know how to talk to parents sensitively about any concerns. You know that you are not able to make a diagnosis but are able to signpost parents to appropriate services. You know that talking to parents about healthy pregnancies is an important part of your role. Find out more from the British Medical Association, and on alcohol and pregnancy: www.bma.org.uk/working-for-change/improving-and-protecting-health/alcohol/alco hol-and-pregnancy and www.chimat.org.uk/beststart/pregnancy.
3	You are familiar with all of the agencies that support children and families affected by prenatal exposure to alcohol, and know where to signpost families to.
4	You create time to discuss your ideas and concerns with other staff to reflect on, discuss and evaluate your practice in relation to children with FASD.
5	You understand that it is important for all staff who work with the child to respond in a similar and consistent way in terms of how staff relate to the child and their parents. You ensure that supply staff and new staff are informed about the needs of each child.
6	You work effectively with other professionals in education, health, social care, and the voluntary and independent sectors.
7	You have attended training in FASD and shared this with all of the staff in your setting.
8	You promote the attitude that all children, including those with special educational needs and disabilities (SEND) and FASD, have the same rights as other children to access all the activities usually provided.
9	You understand that children with FASD will need additional support developing and maintaining positive relationships with their peers and adults, and you provide opportunities in small group and circle time to support this.
10	You understand that children's relationships with their key caregivers are influential in their overall development, and promote parent-child relationships as often as possible.
11	You balance opportunities for children to contribute and share ideas for group work and contribute to group performances, and provide sufficient praise and encouragement to support them in these situations to build confidence.

Number	Competency
12	You use role play, social stories and scripts and photographs to prepare children for events and trips. You make a book with photographs and pictures that helps children to understand and predict what the event or trip might involve and what their participation might mean.
13	You use stories, circle time and social stories, puppets and role play to discuss and explore relationships, emotions and friendships, and you repeat these opportunities frequently.
14	You plan ample opportunities for turn-taking games and circle games to encourage appropriate social interaction with others. You know that children with FASD might find turn-taking difficult and you provide an object (such as a doll or teddy) to pass around at circle time which helps children to remember whose turn it is to speak.
15	You employ 'emotion coaching' strategies to scaffold children's understanding of their feelings and emotions, and to be able to self-regulate and develop autonomy over their responses to difficult situations.

We'd like to have a life instead of the almost daily phone calls from the school about what he has done – or not done – during the school day.

(Parent of a child with FASD, personal communication, Russell, 2013, in
Carpenter et al., 2013: xxiv)

3 Enabling environments

Number	Competency
1	Each child is assigned a key worker who knows the child and family well and with whom the child can build a trusting and caring relationship based upon the concepts of relational pedagogy and professional love.
2	You help children with FASD to develop friendships with other children within and outside the setting whilst respecting each child's social differences and preferences.
3	You observe and assess the potential sensory challenges to children with FASD both indoors and outdoors using the sensory preferences profile in the appendix, and consider how to address these using the sensory passport to personalise your inclusive practice.
4	You understand that children with FASD often require sensory feedback as they have difficulty with sensory integration. This is sometimes perceived as hyperactivity. You ensure that when children with FASD are requested to sit on the carpet in a group (for example, at circle time), they are provided with a marked spot to sit on that is close to the adult speaking to the group, and that they are allowed the use of fidget toys. You reduce visual distractions to a minimum.

(continued)

Number	Competency
5	You understand that children with FASD are easily overwhelmed by sensory stimuli. You develop strategies to reduce the effects of noise, light, touch and sound. For example, you provide rubber caps for the feet of metal chairs to avoid scraping, you ensure that bright lights and loud sounds are reduced as far as possible, and ensure that children with FASD are able to stand at the front or back of any queues. You provide the child with ample warning for any fire drills or other auditory alarms.
6	You understand that some children with FASD will require constant supervision and guidance to keep them and their peers safe from harm due to their impulsive and unpredictable behaviour. You organise the setting with clearly defined spaces/areas for personal equipment and with quiet places of safety for children with FASD.
7	You ensure that activities are well organised, structured and planned, and that, where possible, advance warning is given of any changes to familiar routines in a way that is meaningful to the child with FASD.
8	You combine different methods to communicate with the child to make your message clear (e.g. objects, photos, spoken word, gestures), and teach the child to use appropriate means to initiate communication.
9	You provide individualised, visual supports to ensure that the sequence of activities during the day is understandable and predictable (e.g. objects, photos, pictures, words).
10	You work hard to ensure that you are consistent in your use of language for everyday events and objects (snack, drink, play, story). You aim to ensure that children are not confused by the spoken and written language used or by illustrations. You share communication strategies with parents and carers so language and systems at home and in the early years setting are similar.
11	You adjust your communication by speaking clearly, slowly and calmly, giving the child enough time to process and respond to your instructions.
12	You support children with FASD to select activities both inside and outdoors, taking their interests and social preferences into account.
13	You know how to consider the impact of the physical and social resources in the environment on children's engagement and learning, and adopt a reflective approach to inclusion of children with FASD. For more information, consult the Inquiry Framework from the Complex Learning Difficulties and Disabilities Research Project: http://complexld.ssatrust.org.uk/project-resources/profiling-areas.html.
14	You understand that children with FASD may need a quiet space to allow time to self-regulate and calm them if they become overwhelmed. You provide a space for this which includes headphones, quiet music, cushions, blinds, and activities that calm the child.
15	You know that if there is a child with FASD in the family, there is an increased risk for future pregnancies. You offer guidance and support for families about healthy pregnancies. You know where to find out more information about possible preventative measures: www.euro.who.int/__data/assets/pdf_file/0005/318074/Prevention-harm-caused-alcohol-exposure-pregnancy-.pdf?ua=1.

It was such a battle; I had to be her advocate on so many occasions. We must work together around FASD. The school, the GP [general practitioner], the speech and language therapist and others all worked together but we were so often struggling in the dark. We must demystify FAS [fetal alcohol syndrome] in the same way that we have demystified (and de-stigmatised) so many other conditions and illnesses in the past decade. We also have the big challenge of society itself being willing to change to prevent it in the future.

(Personal communication, Russell, 2013, in Carpenter et al., 2013: xxv)

4 Learning and development

Number	Competency
1	You have a good sense of your own knowledge and understanding of FASD and seek out ways in which you might enhance this.
2	You know that the Early Intervention Foundation maintains a databank of effective early intervention resources and programmes: www.foundationyears.org.uk/eyfs-statutory-framework/. You know that FASD affects children's health and development in a number of ways. Find out more: www.chimat.org.uk/beststart/development.
3	You keep accurate and updated records on the child's progress based on observations of the child, parents' views, and information from other professionals, and you offer parents a central role in the development of the targeted plan. You know that in addition to the EYFS materials (www.foundationyears.org.uk/eyfs-statutory-framework/), you can use the Early Support materials to monitor and assess children's progress in small steps: http://councilfordisabledchildren.org.uk/what-we-do/our-networks/early-support/early-support-resources. You know that children's early health, learning and development are important from a lifespan perspective. Find out more: www.chimat.org.uk/beststart/overview.
4	You understand that a key aim is to promote the child's independence and their inclusion with peers, where appropriate.
5	You understand that children with FASD will often play in different ways from other children, and you teach them how to engage with others gradually and help other children to engage with them.
6	You design play activities to promote each child's development and emotional well-being based on your knowledge of their strengths, interests and challenges in the areas of social and emotional understanding, communication and language, information processing and sensory perception.
7	You understand that group activities such as sharing news or story time can be very difficult for a child with FASD, and take steps to support the child at these times. You make effective use of the child's home-school diary to ensure that you know about the child's home environment and activities in the evenings and weekends to ensure that you can scaffold their memory for activities such as story time and circle time.
8	You know that children with FASD often have greater difficulty in developing eating, drinking, dressing and toileting skills than same-age peers, and you develop and share strategies together with other professionals, parents and carers.

(continued)

Number	Competency
9	You understand that children with FASD might have vision and hearing impairments that need extra support. You know that for vision impairments you can develop children's interests through tactile and sensory experiences such as treasure baskets and sensory rooms. You know that you need to consider the use of lighting, sound and smells in the environment and that you can find out more from: www.rnib.org.uk/services-we-offer-advice-professionals-education-professionals/guidance-teaching-and-learning. You know that children with hearing impairments might need technological support and a number of environmental adaptations, and that you can find out more from: www.ndcs.org.uk/family_support/education_for_deaf_children/education_in_the_early_years/how_nursery_staff.html.
10	You understand that children with FASD can become very stressed and anxious, often by social and sensory demands, and you take steps to reduce or prevent this as it can disrupt and interfere with learning and development.
11	You understand that children with FASD might need extra time to process and respond to instructions. You know that you might need to break instructions and tasks into small steps and that you might need to repeat instructions and key messages/lessons.
12	You know that any group or setting rules might need repeating frequently. You understand that you should not expect a child with FASD to generalise any group or setting rules from one room to another, from one adult to another, or from home to another setting.
13	You understand that children with FASD might find transitions difficult. You carefully prepare children with FASD for minor transitions (for example, between activities, groups, areas). You might signal a transition with music, with signs/symbols or with timers so that the child has sufficient time to shift attention from one task/activity to a new one. A useful tool to help with transitions can be found here: www.pac-uk.org/wp-content/uploads/2016/04/Goodbyes-and-Transitions-V1.1-1.pdf.
14	For more significant transitions such as moving to primary school, you create a detailed profile of the child's skills, strengths and key areas of need to pass on to the next setting, and prepare the child and parents for this transition (for example, visits to the setting; preparing photo journals of the new setting for the child to take home and share with parents; parent discussions/parent visits to the new setting; visits from staff at the new setting).

It was like a new route map. We needed a lot of professionals to mark the roads and deal with the disasters on the way. But now we have the pathway. These are new children and we need new solutions to some very new problems.

(Personal communication, Russell, 2013, in Carpenter et al., 2013: xxv)

Chapter 6

Making human beings human

Relationship-based early childhood inclusion and intervention

Introduction

The role of this chapter is to synthesise the information from previous chapters and organise it in a way that inspires change for the future. The chapter will discuss the role of early childhood inclusion and early childhood intervention for children with Fetal Alcohol Spectrum Disorders (FASD)/who have been exposed prenatally to alcohol, and their families.

In Chapters 1 and 2 it was mentioned that there is a paucity of knowledge about FASD and the effects of prenatal exposure to alcohol (PEA) amongst the early childhood workforce. Chapter 3 focused upon policy in relation to intervention and support for children with FASD and it was noted that this field is currently led by charities with some government contribution from the All-Party Parliamentary Group on FASD. These two factors alone highlight the challenge in providing inclusive early childhood practice and developing appropriate intervention for children with FASD.

As stated in Chapter 3, the most significant challenges for the UK in delivering inclusive early childhood intervention provisions for children with disabilities generally have been:

- Maintaining effective communication with all parties involved;
- Developing a clear understanding of roles and responsibilities between professionals and families;
- Maintaining a high level of professional specialism;
- Developing trust between families and professionals and inter-professionally; and
- Empowering parents and families (Robertson and Messenger, 2010).

These challenges are more pronounced with a condition that is insufficiently understood and under-resourced in terms of workforce development and provision. Early childhood intervention (ECI) in relation to FASD needs to operate broadly at two levels:

- Information for families about healthy pregnancies and sensitive, attuned caregiving; and
- Information and training for the early years workforce about the effects of prenatal exposure to alcohol and how to support young children and their families.

The need for ECI services to be available to children with FASD and their families was stressed in Chapter 3. The question of the content, structure and most effective delivery model of such services needs careful consideration. Dimensions of provision such as workforce development, information and advice provided to families, particular programmes offered to families and location of services are suggested below (Blackburn, 2013).

Suggested ECI approaches for children and families with FASD

1 Professional knowledge and continuing professional development

Professionals involved in ECI programmes should have:

- Understanding of the relationship between women's alcohol consumption and complex psychosocial issues including aspects of women's history and culture. Knowledge of the needs of the whole population, as well as specific groups: school-age children and adolescents, women of child-bearing age, pregnant women, and high-risk women (those with alcohol and poly-substance abuse histories) (Western Australia Department of Health, 2010).
- Training, knowledge and continuing professional development related to assessing and supporting children with FASD and children exposed to maternal alcohol and poly-substance use who are not diagnosed with FASD.
- The ability to suggest and implement a number of intervention programmes based on children's and families' strengths in order to determine which children are developmentally delayed due to lack of appropriate experience and those who will benefit from comprehensive health screening and diagnostic assessment.
- Knowledge of appropriate and available referral pathways (Frances, 2013) and relevant 'touchpoints' (Brazleton, 2003) for children and families to ensure early detection, assessment, diagnosis and support, and that particular attention is provided at sensitive and vulnerable periods (such as times of transition or expected changes in children's pattern of development).
- Knowledge of child neglect and child abuse, and the needs of children who are fostered or adopted. Knowledge of child protection and safeguarding, child development and developmental differences (from conception to age six), and educational and therapeutic approaches suitable for children with a range of medical, physical, neuro-developmental, communication, mental health and sensory needs.
- The ability to view children and families as a diverse group with individual cultural, spiritual and communication needs (Frances and Staggers, 2011), rather than as a homogenous group of service users.
- Interest in and the skills required to work in trans-disciplinary teams to achieve optimal outcomes for children and families from a diverse range of socioeconomic and sociocultural backgrounds.
- Knowledge and skills to work with young children and their families in their natural environments, and to provide counselling and coaching to families and colleagues.
- The ability to reflect on their own practice to assess whether outcomes and goals are being achieved. In particular, the skills and interest to seek new approaches to early detection such as those suggested by Hepper (2013) and De Beer (2008) of observing fetal startle responses *in utero* and observing young children's communication profiles to determine early differences.

- An interest in investigating and implementing new and emerging screening and diagnostic tools (Department of Health, Western Australia, 2010) to ensure windows of opportunity for early detection are not missed. Additional support should be provided for families who already have a child with FASD as this is a risk indicator that further children may be vulnerable (Elliott, 2013).
- The skills to ensure that terminology used for families is accessible and meaningful to them; for example, the terms 'support' and 'advice' are less hostile terms for many families than 'counselling' (Frances and Staggers, 2011).
- The knowledge and skills to develop professional relationships with foster and adoption agencies and understand the needs of birth and adoptive families.
- The ability to promote healthy relationships with families and within families for the benefit of all family members (Moore, 2008).
- The ability to plan transitions from ECI service to mainstream services/other services in a way that minimises disruption and maximises support, clarity and confidence for families (Bruder, 2010).

2 Information/education programmes

Information/education programmes should:

- Be promoted to all interest groups and stakeholders involved in the FASD community (Frances and Staggers, 2011).
- Place families at the heart of provision and include and consult with them on all aspects of ECI services offered to them in ways that demonstrate dignity and respect as well as inclusion and participation (a key aspect of this is observing children's rights to have their voices heard in line with United Nations Conventions on the Rights of the Child).
- Inform families about healthy pregnancies and maternal health issues in the pregnancy and postnatal periods, including healthy breast-feeding (Allen, 2011; NOFAS-UK, 2010).
- Inform families and the professionals who support them about the effects of prenatal alcohol exposure and fetal exposure to other substances (Blackburn et al., 2012).
- Provide information for families about child development, the developmental implications of FASD for their child/children, including the importance of early attachment and caregiver-child interactions (Cuthbert et al., 2012).

3 Assessment, intervention, education, therapy and related services

Therapies and other services should:

- Provide a range of therapeutic care and educational services to address the holistic learning and developmental needs of children with FASD across developmental domains. This would ideally be delivered through an interdisciplinary approach and be based on the child's strengths and successes as well as needs. There should be a focus on children's rights and potential to develop their identity and personality within their diverse communities. Improvements in children's attention span, sensitivity to touch and capacity to play in productive and educational ways (Kleinfeld, 1993) have been noted as a result of particular therapeutic interventions in children's early years.

- Commence as soon as possible, either during pregnancy or after birth (Murphy, 1993: 191), in order to address children's sensory needs. The objective should be to identify and promote activities that prevent the child from becoming over- or under-stimulated both mentally and physically, by increasing tolerance to touch as well as tolerance for noise in the environment through a staged introduction to noises when children are relaxed.
- Value families' contribution to interventions and programmes delivered by play therapists and teachers working together which will improve the sustainability of interventions that can be embedded within a family context and used to help generalise learning from school/ECI settings to home (Hinde, 1993: 131–132).
- Provide comprehensive health screening services for pregnant women and infants as well as early diagnostic services (BMA, 2007; Kleinfeld and Wescott, 1993).
- Provide opportunities for parents and carers (and children) to socialise and seek advice from and support each other in a safe, supportive environment (Frances and Staggers, 2011).
- Provide advocacy services for children and families (Frances and Staggers, 2011).
- Sensitively support all families and be aware of the particular needs of those who abuse alcohol (and other substances) (Cuthbert et al., 2012).
- Provide counselling services for families in relation to family issues. This would include birth families, foster carers and adoptive families, and address any feelings of guilt that may be evident in birth families.
- Provide mental health services (Cuthbert et al., 2012).
- Provide early childhood care and education services for children which identify their strengths, successes and needs, provide developmentally and contextually appropriate opportunities to enable children to enjoy positive early years experiences (Whitebread and Bingham, 2011).
- Provide community-based educational services in order for the neighbourhood systems that children inhabit to understand the needs of children and families affected by FASD.

The provision of these services in locations convenient for family access delivered by professionals who can empathise with and respect a range of family needs and structures should be a priority for national government and local authorities. The discussions throughout this book about children's learning and development have focused on the importance of relationships. A relationship-based early childhood intervention service that places the child-parent relationship at the centre of its provision is called for in this chapter.

Relationship-based ECI services

ECI services should operate from the perspective that every child, no matter what developmental challenges they face, will learn and grow through the intervention of skilled therapists and informed parents/caregivers. Ideally ECI services should be based on the following principles (www.championcentre.org.nz):

- They should be relational – focused on building strong relationships between children and their social world;
- They should be family-centred – the focus should be on the family as the child's most important context;

- They should be strengths-based – building on the child's strengths to develop further skills;
- They should be ecological – the contexts in which children function include families and broader social and political contexts in which children function;
- They should be reflective – reviewing, questioning, learning, thinking and discussion between staff; and
- They should be underpinned by scientific evidence about international best practice and a model of advocacy.

Professionals working in ECI services should hold high aspirations for children and families and this should include aspirations for successful parent-child relationships. Professionals should engage in respectful professional interactions and relationships with children and families. Integrated professional working, effective and timely communication between professionals and families, and personalised programmes for children are also important dimensions (Blackburn, 2015, 2016). The notions of relational pedagogy and professional love have been suggested in previous chapters of this book as important dimensions of professional caregiving. These concepts include the following dimensions of professional caregiving in the context of ECI services:

- A reflective, empathetic, professional approach;
- Respect for family patterns, interactions and priorities;
- Celebration of each child's (and family's) strengths and competencies;
- A willingness and ability to explain both *why* and *how* interventions are chosen and model these to parents in an empowering way;
- Enthusiasm to work with children within the context of families;
- The ability to think contextually and holistically about children;
- Enthusiasm for a relationship-based model and ethos; and
- The ability to take account of other professional disciplines.

In addition, at the contextual and interpersonal levels, the following should be evident:

- Professionals should have permission and the opportunity to build relationships with and love children/families;
- Recognition of the need for balance between professional disciplinary specialism and shared interdisciplinary perspectives;
- Recognition of the value of theory to practice in ECI services;
- Opportunities to give families time to talk with professionals and other families;
- Opportunities are necessary for professional joint training within the context of teamwork; and
- Professionals need permission and opportunities to support transitions within programmes, between programmes and into school.

However, services should be legislated for, quality assured and part of a coordinated, integrated model of provision and delivery which are prioritised at national, local and community levels.

These characteristics of relational pedagogy (or relationship-based services) and professional love contextualised within a coordinated, legislative and quality-assured ECI service are conceptualised in Figure 6.1.

Applying relational pedagogy and professional love to early childhood intervention services

Characteristics of relationship-based early childhood intervention services

Contextual and interpersonal

➤ Legislation and QA for the recognition of the importance of a strengths-based, ecological, relational, reflective, family-centred approach to provision of ECI services

➤ Permission and opportunity to build relationships with and love children/families

➤ Recognition of balance between professional disciplinary specialism and shared interdisciplinary perspectives

➤ Recognition of the value of theory to practice in ECI services

➤ Opportunities to give families time to talk with professionals and other families

➤ Opportunities for professional joint training

➤ Opportunities for professional development within the context of teamwork

➤ Permission to support transitions within programmes, between programmes and into school

© Carolyn Blackburn, 2016

Individual and intrapersonal

➤ Reflective empathetic approach

➤ Respect for family patterns, interactions and priorities

➤ Celebration of each child's (and families') strengths and competencies

➤ Ability to explain both *why* and *how* interventions are chosen and model to parents in an empowering way

➤ Enthusiasm to work with children within the context of families

➤ Ability to think contextually and holistically about children

➤ Enthusiasm for the relationship-based model and ethos

➤ Ability to take account of other professional disciplines

Resulting outcomes for children families, communities and societies

Individual and intrapersonal

Professionals:

➤ Place parent-child relationship at the centre of programmes and individual plans

➤ Acknowledge and value the contribution of other professional disciplines

➤ Reflect critically on research and theory

➤ Be open to alternative ways to develop practice

➤ Value the development of teams balanced with professional development

Children:

➤ Progression and long term social and educational success

Families:

➤ Parents know, understand and love their child

➤ Parent advocates

➤ Parental confidence (in themselves and their children)

➤ Peer support

Contextual and interpersonal

➤ Effective and timely communication between professionals and families

➤ Interdisciplinary meetings after EI sessions to discuss children's progress and development

➤ Pedagogy of listening, waiting and personalisation

➤ Responsiveness to family patterns, interactions, routines, stressors and strengths

➤ Engaged families

➤ Actively participating children (and later young people)

➤ Knowledge transferred to family and wider settings

➤ Community and societal understanding and tolerance

➤ Children (and young people) with disabilities make a positive contribution to community and society

➤ Inclusive, diverse, rich communities and societies

Figure 6.1 Applying relational pedagogy and professional love to early childhood intervention services

The benefits of this can be measured at the individual level in terms of resilience, well-being and long-term success, and at the community and society levels in terms of economic gains and more diverse, inclusive and rich society. To return to Bronfenbrenner (1979), this allows the integration of theory, policy and practice from what *is currently inclusion* for children with FASD to *what could be inclusion* for FASD when the multiple, integrative contexts in which those children grow and develop work in harmony.

Conclusion

This chapter has summarised the current UK situation with regard to ECI for children with FASD. Suggestions for ECI provision for the future have been made. Reducing the number of children born prenatally exposed to alcohol must surely be a primary intervention goal for all governments, followed by positive early childhood inclusion and intervention programmes for children and their families. This should yield long-term benefits for children, families, communities and society.

Acknowledgements

Parts of this chapter have been published previously in C. Blackburn (2013). Walking through a moonless night: Fetal alcohol spectrum disorders and early childhood intervention. In B. Carpenter, C. Blackburn and J. Egerton (eds), *Fetal alcohol spectrum disorders: Interdisciplinary perspectives*. London: Routledge.

Reflecting on your practice

- What will you do now to improve the availability of provision and services for children with FASD?
- Could you organise an awareness-raising initiative in your local area?
- Could you provide training and support for other early childhood providers/professionals?
- Could you collaborate with other interdisciplinary professionals in your area to form an action group?
- Could you lobby your local MP?

Appendix A

Sensory preferences profile

Child's name:

Child's date of birth:

Date profile completed:

Name of setting:

Please tick the most appropriate box

Section 1 – Balance (vestibular) system (movement-based senses)

Does the child frequently seek motion (spin around, rock, jump)?	Y ☐	N ☐
Are they always on the go (moving around, restless)?	Y ☐	N ☐
Do they move their limbs around even when seated?	Y ☐	N ☐
Do they prefer to be active?	Y ☐	N ☐
Do they prefer activities where they avoid movement (e.g. TV, tablet)?	Y ☐	N ☐
Do they like repetitive movements?	Y ☐	N ☐

Section 2 – Body awareness (proprioception) system (body judgement and sense of space)

Does the child have poor motor control (unsteady gait, unable to fasten zips)?	Y ☐	N ☐
Do they tire easily?	Y ☐	N ☐
Do they have poor posture?	Y ☐	N ☐
Does physical activity: Distress them? ☐ Relax them? ☐ Have no known effect? ☐		
Are they sensitive to people invading their personal space?	Y ☐	N ☐
Do they chew clothing or other items?	Y ☐	N ☐
Do they find using stairs difficult?	Y ☐	N ☐

Section 3 – Smell (olfactory) system (sensory experiences relating to smells)

Is the child drawn to specific smells (e.g. flowers, metal, earth, citrus, foods)?	Y ☐	N ☐

If so, please give examples of these specific smells: _____

_____

Do they appear to find smells overpowering?	Y ☐	N ☐

If so, please give examples of these specific smells: _____

_____

Do they appear not to notice strong smells that others do or avoid them? Y ☐ N ☐

Do they smear faeces? Y ☐ N ☐

Section 4 – Taste (gustatory) system (preferences on textures and flavours)

From the viewpoint of using food as a reward, what tastes does the child like and find rewarding (e.g. sweet, sour, bitter, smooth, rough, soft, hard, crunchy, strong or bland taste)? Please give specific examples if possible: _____

_____

What food do they avoid? _____

_____

Do they have any preferences regarding presentation of food (e.g. separated)? _____

_____

Section 5 – Sight (visual) system (visual sensory experiences)

Does the child like or dislike strong colours, fibres, shiny objects? Like ☐ Dislike ☐

Do they have a favourite, calming colour? Y ☐ N ☐
If so, what? _____

Do they prefer dark or light environments? Dark ☐ Light ☐

Do they self-stimulate their eyesight (e.g. flicking fingers, pressing eye lids)? Y ☐ N ☐

Do they cover their eyes for apparently no reason? Y ☐ N ☐

Do they remove stimuli from their environment (e.g. shut curtains, remove lights)? Y ☐ N ☐

Do they have preferences or fears regarding how people look (hair up/down, hats, jewellery, male/female)? _____

_____

Section 6 – Hearing (auditory) system (preferences relating to noise and sounds)

Does the child like or dislike noise around them? Like ☐ Dislike ☐

Do they make loud noises? Y ☐ N ☐

Do they like listening to music? Y ☐ N ☐

If so, what type? _____

Are they distracted by 'white noise' (e.g. background noises, buzzing lights)? Y ☐ N ☐

Do they prefer silence? Y ☐ N ☐

Do they prefer people to talk quietly to them? Y ☐ N ☐

Section 7 – Touch (tactile) system (type of touch experiences they prefer)

Does the child seek out or avoid touch? Seeks ☐ Avoids ☐

If they seek it, do they prefer: Deep pressure ☐ Light ☐

Do they like having messy hands? Y ☐ N ☐

Do they like having pressure around them
(e.g. tight clothing, weights, being tucked up tightly in bed)? Y ☐ N ☐

Do they like playing with water? Y ☐ N ☐

What textures do they appear to like (e.g. rough, smooth, soft, hard, bumpy)? _____
_____

What textures do they appear to dislike? _____
_____

Do they prefer warm or cold temperatures? Warmer ☐ Cooler ☐

Section 8 – Communication (efficient ways to speak with the child and inform them)

Does the child use: Verbal communication ☐

Makaton ☐

Visual prompts ☐

Object of reference ☐

Other (please specify) _____

How many words in a sentence do they understand? _____

Do they have difficulties interpreting verbal communication? Y ☐ N ☐

Does saying their name help them to know that you are speaking to them? Y ☐ N ☐

Does their communication level depend on their anxiety Y ☐ N ☐
(e.g. does it decrease if they are stressed?)?

If yes, please give more details on how this is affected and proactive ways you use to overcome
this: _____
_____

Are they sensitive to eye contact, especially when stressed? Y ☐ N ☐

Section 9 – Transition and movement

C1. Does the child have difficulty moving from one task to another? Y ☐ N ☐

C2. Do they have difficulty multi-tasking? Y ☐ N ☐

C3. What works well when preparing the child to move onto a new activity or one they may be anxious about?

_____

_____

C4. What does not work well when preparing the child for a new activity, especially one they may be anxious about?

_____

_____

C5. How does the child cope with demands?

_____

_____

C6. How does the child cope with waiting for something (e.g. are they restless, do they need something to occupy the time, have no difficulty with waiting)?

_____

_____

C7. How does the child cope with boredom and tiredness (e.g. they have no difficulty with this, they become agitated and stressed, or they need something to occupy their time)?

_____

_____

C8. What are the best distractions for the child (e.g. food, games, TV, DVDs, music, talking)?

_____

_____

Adapted from materials developed by:

Charlotte Gayson, Andrea Page, Andrew A. McDonnell and Nicola Vanes on behalf of Birmingham City University, Studio III and NIHR/Wellcome Trust Clinical Research Facility, Birmingham Children's Hospital.

Publication: Page, A., Gayson, C., Vanes, N., Ashmore, P. and McDonnell, A. (2016, in press) Sensing what's important: Determining parental preferences of children with Hunters Syndrome/Sanfilippo syndrome for when they are receiving treatment in hospital. _RCNi Journal Learning Disability Practice._

Appendix B
Sensory passport

Child's name:

Date:

Setting:

Below is a list of recommendations and approaches to consider based on the information gathered from the sensory preferences profile

Sensory system	Seeks out	Avoids	No known effect	Child's preference/notes
Balance (vestibular)	If the child enjoys movement and this relaxes them then time outside or where they have space should be promoted so they can make the most of the space and burn energy If the child likes repetitive movements, add activities that require this type of movement, e.g. colouring, games, puzzles	If the child avoids movement or appears clumsy by bumping into things then plan activities that do not require fast movements such as playing ICT or puzzles Let the child complete activities at their own pace Break down movements into small steps	If there are no preferences then provide options for the child to choose from and keep a record of what you use and how the child responds	*Please cross out the recommendations or considerations that do not apply for the child* *Any additional comments can go in this section* _____ _____ _____ _____
Body awareness (proprioception)	If the child appears to have good motor control and posture then no necessary changes may need to take place	Allow the child time. If they have poor motor control then do not have only small, fiddly objects in the room as this may distress/frustrate them. Ensure they will be comfortable if they have poor posture when sitting or lying	If there are no preferences then provide options for the child to choose from and keep a record of what you use and how the child responds	*Please cross out the recommendations or considerations that do not apply for the child* *Any additional comments can go in this section* _____ _____ _____ _____

(continued)

Sensory system	Seeks out	Avoids	No known effect	Child's preference/notes
Smell (olfactory)	If there are specific smells that the child is drawn to then ensure that these smells are available for the child. Focus on positive smells, distracting from negative ones If they do not appear to notice smells, they have a low registration as opposed to not being interested	If there are specific smells that the child always avoids and finds overpowering then ensure that these smells are not present when the child enters the room. The room should be fragrance-free if possible. Corridors and entrances/exits should also be fragrance free where possible	If there are no preferences then provide options for the child to choose from and keep a record of what you use and how the child responds	*Please cross out the recommendations or considerations that do not apply for the child* *Any additional comments can go in this section* _____ _____ _____ _____ _____
Taste (gustatory)	Have the child's favourite taste available as a reward/distraction	Ensure that the child is not given anything they do not like/avoids If they have their food separated on a plate, ensure this is how food is presented	Keep a record of what you use and how the child responds	*Please cross out the recommendations or considerations that do not apply for the child* *Any additional comments can go in this section* _____ _____ _____ _____ _____

Sensory system	Seeks out	Avoids	No known effect	Child's preference/notes
Sight (visual)	If the child is drawn to flashing, bright objects and stimulates their eyesight then ensure that objects and activities are in the room that promote this – bright colours, hologram on the wall, torches Use art with bright colours and complicated patterns. Ideal equipment: projector, fibre optics, carpet with lights, ultraviolet lights, ceiling lights, cushions, books, TV	If the child appears to avoid such stimulation then try to use dimmer switches for the lights, black-out tents, blinds are down and the room in general has low stimulation. This means ensuring that only the activities that would be of interest to the child are in the room, and all others removed	If there are no preferences then provide options for the child. Do not have an empty room, or a chaotic room with too many options. If the child has a favourite colour (especially a calming one), then items that are this colour should be present, and staff should possibly wear or have an object in this colour. Keep a record of what you use and how the child responds	*Please cross out the recommendations or considerations that do not apply for the child* *Any additional comments can go in this section* _____ _____ _____ _____ _____
Hearing (auditory)	If the child likes noise around them then ensure objects that make noises are in the room, ensure music they like is played for them Stereo, noisy/colour wheel, rattling baton, bell, small talking bus, TV	If the child prefers a quiet environment then ensure all noisy objects are out of the room. Try to let the child have the room on their own. Shut windows and doors to remove external noises. Offer earplugs/personal headphones	If there are no preferences then provide options for the child. Play music if they like it. Have a mix of sensory objects in the room – silent and noisy ones. Keep a record of what you use and how the child responds	*Please cross out the recommendations or considerations that do not apply for the child* *Any additional comments can go in this section* _____ _____ _____ _____ _____

(continued)

Sensory system	Seeks out	Avoids	No known effect	Child's preference/notes
Touch (tactile)	If the child seeks tactile stimulation, ensure various objects are available in the room that match their preferences – rough, smooth, soft, hard (e.g. netting, play dough)

If they like deep pressure/tactile stimulation then keep this in mind and have activities in the room that may meet this need

If they prefer soft touch, then have options such as feathers they can brush against their skin. If they enjoy water play, offer this as an option. Plan for mixed-texture dough tubs to be available | If the child avoids touch as this is too overwhelming for them, ensure awareness of this and try to avoid the child being placed in the middle of queues for hygiene and transition times. Try to seat the child on the edge of the carpet for carpet activities rather than in the middle

Approach the child from the front and inform them so they can see you and expect any touch occurring

Let the child initiate the touch if possible | If there are no preferences then provide options for the child. Have a mix of sensory tactile objects in the room

Ensure the temperature is at a medium setting. Keep a record of what you use and how the child responds | *Please cross out the recommendations or considerations that do not apply for the child*

Any additional comments can go in this section

_____

_____

_____

_____

_____ |

© 2017 Carolyn Blackburn, *Developing Inclusive Practice for Young Children with Fetal Alcohol Spectrum Disorders*, Routledge

B – Communication

Verbal	Non-verbal
When stressed, children are less likely to be able to process a lot of information. In these times, speak to the child using short, simple communication	Makaton, cue cards, pictures, object of reference
	Use of 'now and next' cards to communicate what will happen
If they prefer quiet, soft voices then please use this	Develop social stories for their visits. Social stories are ways to help children with learning difficulties develop greater social understanding
If the child calms with humour then please use this method when communicating to reduce any stress	Be aware of non-verbal body language; avoid aggressive stances such as folded arms and appearing distracted (this also includes maintaining personal space); do not invade the child's space if it is not necessary, and be mindful and reassuring if this is needed when talking to children
	If the child likes the use of computers and technology, then consider using these as a medium for communication
Comments about the child's verbal skills/techniques:	Comments about the child's non-verbal skills/techniques:

C – Transition and movement

C1. If the child has difficulty moving from one task to another, then ensure all communication methods that are appropriate for the child are used – pictures, social stories, object of reference. This allows the child to predict the next task and this is easier to understand when stressed, aiding the transition. Ensure the task they are completing is finished before another demand is added.

C2. If the child cannot multi-task, giving them more than one task at a time will cause them stress and therefore may lead to behaviours of concern. Consequently, only provide one demand at a time, ensuring the child has finished any task in hand before being asked to do another one. Also make sure the child is attending to you when you are communicating with them.

C3. What works well when preparing the child for a new activity/one that causes stress:

_____
_____

C4. What does not work well when preparing the child for a new activity/one that causes stress:

_____
_____

C5. How the child copes with demands:

_____
_____

C6. How the child copes with waiting:

_____
_____

C7. How the child copes with tiredness and boredom:

C8. The best distractions for this child are:

Adapted from materials developed by:

Charlotte Gayson, Andrea Page, Andrew A. McDonnell and Nicola Vanes on behalf of Birmingham City University, Studio III and NIHR/Wellcome Trust Clinical Research Facility, Birmingham Children's Hospital.

Publication: Page, A., Gayson, C., Vanes, N., Ashmore, P. and McDonnell, A. (2016, in press) Sensing what's important: Determining parental preferences of children with Hunters Syndrome/Sanfilippo syndrome for when they are receiving treatment in hospital. *RCNi Journal Learning Disability Practice.*

References

Abel, E.L. and Hannigan, J.H. (1995). Maternal risk factors in fetal alcohol syndrome: Provocative and permissive influences. *Neurotoxicology and Teratology*, 17: 445–462. PMID: 7565491.

Ainsworth, M.D.S., Biehar, M.C., Waters, E. and Wall, S. (1978). *Patterns of attachment: A psychological study of the strange situation.* Hillsdale, NJ: Erlbaum.

Allen, G. (2011). *Early intervention: The next steps. An independent report to Her Majesty's Government.* London: HM Government.

Astley, S.J., Stachowiak, J., Clarren, S.K. and Clausen, C. (2002). Application of the fetal alcohol syndrome facial photographic screening tool in a foster care population. *Journal of Pediatrics*, 141(5): 712–717.

Aynsley-Green, A. (2016). Foreword in British Medical Association, *Alcohol and pregnancy: Preventing and managing fetal alcohol spectrum disorders* (pp. ix). London: British Medical Association.

Baldock, P., Fitzgerald, D. and Kay, J. (2013). *Understanding early years policy*, third edition. London: Sage Publications.

Blackburn, C. (2010). *Facing the challenge and shaping the future for primary and secondary aged students with foetal alcohol spectrum disorders (FAS-eD Project).* London: National Organisation on Fetal Alcohol Syndrome (UK).

Blackburn, C. (2013). Walking through a moonless night: Fetal alcohol spectrum disorders and early childhood intervention. In B. Carpenter, C. Blackburn and J. Egerton (eds), *Fetal alcohol spectrum disorders: Interdisciplinary perspectives* (pp. 102–122). London: Routledge.

Blackburn, C. (2015). *Relationship-based early intervention services for children with complex needs: Lessons from New Zealand.* Available: www.wcmt.org.uk/sites/default/files/report-docum ents/Blackburn%20C%20Report%202015%20Final.pdf (accessed 27 September 2016).

Blackburn, C. (2016). Relationship-based early intervention services for children with complex needs: Lessons from New Zealand. *International Journal of Birth and Parent Education*, 3(3): 27–30.

Blackburn, C. (2016). Early childhood inclusion in the United Kingdom. *Infants & Young Children*, 29(3): 239–246.

Blackburn, C. (2016). Relationship-based early intervention services: Lessons from New Zealand. *Journal of Children's Services*, 11(4): 330–344. Available: http://www.emeraldinsight.com/doi/full/10.1108/JCS-04-2016-0008

Blackburn, C. and Aubrey, C. (2016). Policy-to-practice context to delays and difficulties in the acquisition of speech, language and communication in early years. *International Journal of Early Years Education*, 24(4): 414–434.

Blackburn, C., Carpenter, B. and Egerton, J. (2010). Shaping the future for children with foetal alcohol spectrum disorders. *Support for Learning*, 25(3): 139–146.

Blackburn, C., Carpenter, B. and Egerton, J. (2012). *Educating children and young people with fetal alcohol spectrum disorders.* London: Routledge.

Blackburn, C.M., Spencer, N.J. and Read, J.M. (2010). Prevalence of childhood disability and the characteristics and circumstances of disabled children in the UK. *BMC Pediatrics*, 10(21).

Blackburn, C. and Whitehurst, T. (2010). Foetal alcohol spectrum disorders (FASD): Raising awareness in early years settings. *British Journal of Special Education*, 27(3): 122–129.

Blackburn, C. and Williams, P. (2013). *Survey of European Birth Mothers Network: FASD and early childhood intervention*. Unpublished.

Blair, T. (1999). Beveridge revisited: A welfare state for the 21st century. In R. Walker (ed.), *Ending child poverty* (pp. 7–18). Bristol: Policy Press.

Bowen, J., Gibson, F. and Hand, P. (2002). Educational outcome at 8 years for children who were born extremely prematurely: A controlled study. *Journal of Paediatric and Child Health*, 38(5): 438–444.

Bowlby, J. (1969). *Attachment and loss, volume 1: Attachment*. London: Hogarth Press.

Brazelton, T.B. and Sparrow, J. (2003). *Touchpoints model of development*. Boston: Brazleton Touchpoints Center.

British Medical Association (BMA) (2007). *Fetal alcohol spectrum disorders: A guide for healthcare professionals*. London: British Medical Association.

British Medical Association (BMA) (2016). *Alcohol and pregnancy: Preventing and managing fetal alcohol spectrum disorders*. London: British Medical Association.

Bronfenbrenner, U. (1979). *The ecology of human development*. Cambridge: Harvard University Press.

Bronfenbrenner, U. (1992). Ecological systems theory. In R. Basta (ed.), *Six theories of child development: Revised formulations and current issues* (pp. 187–249). Philadelphia, PA: Kingsley.

Bronfenbrenner, U. (1993). The ecology of cognitive development: Research models and fugitive findings. In R.H. Wozniak and K.W. Fisher (eds), *Development in context: Acting and thinking in specific environments* (pp. 3–44). Hillsdale, NJ: Erlbaum.

Bronfenbrenner, U. (2001). The bioecology theory of human development. In N.J. Smelser and P.B. Baltes (eds), *International encyclopedia of the social and behavioral sciences*, vol. 10 (pp. 6963–6970). Newnes.

Bruder, M.B. (2010). Early childhood intervention: A promise to children and families for their future. *Exceptional Children*, 76(3): 339–355.

Bruner, J. (1983). *Child's talk: Learning to use language*. Oxford: Oxford University Press.

Carel, C. (2016). Virtue without excellence, excellence without health. *Aristotelian Society Supplementary Volume*, xc: 237–253.

Carmichael Olson, H. and Gurgess, D.M. (1997). Early intervention for children prenatally exposed to alcohol and other drugs. In M.J. Guralnick (ed.), *The effectiveness of early intervention*. Baltimore: Paul H. Brookes Publishing.

Carpenter, B. (2005). Real prospects for early childhood intervention: Family aspirations and professional implications. In B. Carpenter and J. Egerton (eds), *Early childhood intervention: International perspectives, national initiatives and regional practice* (pp. 13–38). Coventry: West Midlands SEN Regional Partnership.

Carpenter, B., Blackburn, C. and EgertonJ. (2013). *Fetal alcohol spectrum disorders: Interdisciplinary perspectives*. London: Routledge.

Carpenter, B., Egerton, J., Brooks, T., Cockbill, B., Fotheringham, J. and Rawson, H. (2011). *The Complex Learning Difficulties and Disabilities Research Project: Developing pathways to personalised learning*. London: Specialist Schools and Academies Trust.

Carpenter, B., Egerton, J., Cockbill, B., Bloom, T., Fotheringham, J., Rawson, H. and Thistle-thwaite, J. (2015). *Engaging learners with complex learning difficulties and disabilities: A resource book for teachers and teaching assistants*. London: Routledge.

Cassidy, J. (1999). The nature of a child's ties. In J. Cassidy and P.R. Shaver, *Handbook of attachment: Theory, research and clinical applications* (pp. 3–20). New York: Guilford Press.

Catterick, M. and Curran, L. (2014). *Understanding fetal alcohol spectrum disorder: A guide for parents, carers and professionals*. London: Jessica Kingsley Publishers.

Champion, P. (2010). In *Complex Learning Difficulties and Disabilities Research Project attachment information sheet*. London: Specialist Schools and Academies Trust. Available: http://complexld. ssatrust.org.uk/project-information.html

Chasnoff, I.J. (2010). *The mystery of risk: Drugs, alcohol, pregnancy and the vulnerable child*. Chicago: NTI Upstream.

Claussen, A.H. and Crittenden, P.M. (2000). Maternal sensitivity. In P.M. Crittenden and A.H. Claussen (eds), *The organisation of attachment relationships* (pp. 115–124). New York: Cambridge University Press.

Crittenden, P.M. (1988). *CARE-Index Manual*, third revision. Unpublished manuscript, Miami, FL.

Cuthbert, C., Raynes, G. and Stanley, K. (2011). *All babies count: Prevention and protection for vulnerable babies*. National Society for the Prevention of Cruelty to Children (NSPCC).

Davis, H.A. (2003). Conceptualizing the role and influence of student–teacher relationships on children's social and cognitive development . *Educational Psychologist*, 38(4): 207–234.

Davis, H., Day, C. and Bidmead, C. (2002). *Working in partnership with parents: The parent advisor model*. London: Harcourt Assessment.

De Beer, M.M. (2008). *Communication profiles of a group of young children (0–5) with Foetal Alcohol Spectrum Disorders*. Unrestricted M. Communication Pathology Dissertation. South Africa: University of Pretoria.

Department for Children and Families and Department of Health (DOH) (2008). *The Child Health Promotion Programme: Pregnancy and the first five years of life*. London: Department of Health.

Department for Children Schools and Families (DCSF) (2006). *Common assessment framework*. Nottingham: DSCF.

Department for Education (DfE) (2011). *Support and aspiration: A new approach to special educational needs and disability*. Norwich: The Stationery Office.

Department for Education (DfE) (2013). *Early years outcomes: A non-statutory guide for practitioners and inspectors to help inform understanding of child development through the early years*. Available: www.gov.uk/government/publications/early-years-outcomes (accessed 22 January 2014).

Department for Education (DfE) (2014). *Statutory framework for the Early Years Foundation Stage*. Available: www.foundationyears.org.uk/eyfs-2014/ (accessed 21 September 2016).

Department for Education (DfE), Department for Business, Innovation and Skills, Department for Work and Pensions (DWP), Department of Health (DOH) and Ministry of Justice (2014). *Children and Families Act*. Available: www.legislation.gov.uk/ukpga/2014/6/contents/enacted (accessed 21 September 2016).

Department for Education (DfE) and Department of Health (DOH) (2011). *Supporting families in the foundation years*.

Department for Education (DfE) and Department of Health (DOH) (2015). *Special educational needs (SEN) code of practice: Statutory guidance for organisations who work with and support children and young people with SEN*.

Department for Education and Employment (DfEE) (1997). *Excellence for all children: Meeting special educational needs*. London: HMSO.

Department for Education and Skills (DfES) (2001). *Special educational needs code of practice*. Nottingham: DfES Publications.

Department for Education and Skills (DfES) (2002). *Birth to three matters: A framework to support children in their earliest years*. London: DfES.

Department for Education and Skills (DfES) (2004a). *Early support programme family pack and professional guidance*. Nottingham: DfES Publications.

Department for Education and Skills (DfES) (2004b). *Removing barriers to achievement: The government's strategy for SEN*. Nottingham: DfES Publications.

Department for Education and Skills (DfES) and Department of Health (DOH) (2003). *Together from the start: Practical guidance for professionals working with disabled children (birth to third birthday) and their families*. Nottingham: DfES Publications.

Department of Health, Western Australia (2010). *Fetal alcohol spectrum disorder model of care.* Perth: Health Networks Branch, Department of Health, Western Australia.

Department for Work and Pensions (DWP) and Department for Education (DfE) (2011). *A new approach to child poverty: Tackling the causes of disadvantage and transforming families' lives.* Norwich: The Stationery Office.

Dockrell, J. and McShane, J. (1992). *Children's learning difficulties: A cognitive approach.* Oxford: Blackwell Publishers.

Dunst, C.J. and Trivette, C.M. (1997). Early intervention with young at-risk children and their families. In R. Ammerman and M. Hersen (eds), *Handbook of prevention and treatment with children and adolescents: Intervention in the real world* (pp. 157–180). New York: Wiley.

Egerton, J. (2013). A step in time: Fetal alcohol spectrum disorders and transition to adulthood. In B. Carpenter, C. Blackburn and J. Egerton (eds), *Fetal alcohol spectrum disorders: Interdisciplinary perspectives* (pp. 141–158). London: Routledge.

Elliott, E. (2013). Fetal alcohol spectrum disorders: Australian perspectives. In B. Carpenter, C. Blackburn and J. Egerton (eds), *Fetal alcohol spectrum disorders: Interdisciplinary perspectives* (pp. 294–305). London: Routledge.

Emerson, E. and Hatton, C. (2005). *The socio-economic circumstances of families supporting a child at risk of disability in Britain in 2002.* Lancaster: University of Lancaster.

Field, F. (2010). *The foundation years: Preventing poor children becoming poor adults. The report of the Independent Review on Poverty and Life Chances.* Available: www.frankfield.com/campaigns/poverty-and-life-changes.aspx (accessed 21 September 2016).

Fisher, R. (1998). *Early Child Development and Care*, 141: 1–15.

Frances, K. (2013). Fetal alcohol spectrum disorders: Knowledge and referral pathways in early childhood settings in Western Australia. In B. Carpenter, C. Blackburn and J. Egerton (eds), *Fetal alcohol spectrum disorders: Interdisciplinary perspectives* (pp. 91–101). London: Routledge.

Frances, K. and Staggers, S. (2011). *Evaluation of Palmerston Association yarning and parenting program for parents and children experiencing drug and alcohol problems.* Perth, Western Australia: National Drug Research Institute, Curtin University.

Fredericks, J.A., Blumenfeld, P.C. and Paris, A.H. (2004). Student engagement: Potential of the concept, state of the evidence. *Review of Educational Research*, 74(1): 59–109.

Freiler, T. (2008). Learning through the body. In S. Merriam (ed.), *New directions for adult and continuing education: no. 119* (pp. 37–48). San Francisco: Jossey-Bass, Wiley.

Goswami, U. (2008). *Learning difficulties: Future challenges. Mental Capital and Wellbeing Project.* London: HMSO: Government Office for Science.

Goswami, U. (2011). Cognitive neuroscience and learning and development. In J. Moyles, J. Georgeson and J. Payler (eds), *Beginning teaching beginning learning in early years and primary education.* Maidenhead: Open University Press.

Gottman, J., Katz, L. and Hooven, C. (1996). Parental meta-emotion philosophy and the emotional life of families: Theoretical models and preliminary data. *Journal of Family Psychology*, 10(3): 243–268.

Gottman, J., Katz, L. and Hooven, C. (1997). *Meta-emotion: How families communicate emotionally.* New Jersey: Lawrence Erlbaum Associates.

Graziano, P.A., Reavis, R.D., Keane, S.P. and Calkins, S.D. (2007). Emotion regulation and children's early academic success. *Journal of School Psychology*, 45(1): 3–19.

Guralnick, M. (1997). Second generation research in the field of early intervention. In M.J. Guralnick (ed.), *The effectiveness of early intervention* (pp. 3–20). Baltimore, MD: Brookes.

Guralnick, M. (2004). Introduction: What is early intervention? In M. Feldman (ed.), *Early intervention: The essential readings* (pp. 1–4). Oxford: Blackwell Publishing.

Guralnick, M. (2005). *The developmental systems approach to early intervention.* Baltimore, MD: Paul H. Brookes.

Havighurst, S.S., Wilson, K.R., Harley, A.E., Kehoe, C., Efron, D. and Prior, M.R. (2013). 'Tuning into kids': Reducing young children's behavior problems using an emotion coaching parenting program. *Journal of Child Psychiatry and Human Development*, 44(2): 247–264.

Henricson, C. (2012). *A revolution in family policy: Where should we go from here?* Bristol, UK: The Policy Press.

Hepper, P. (2013). Fetal behaviour and the effect of maternal alcohol consumption. In B. Carpenter, C. Blackburn and J. Egerton (eds), *Fetal alcohol spectrum disorders: Interdisciplinary perspectives* (pp. 53–64). London: Routledge.

Her Majesty's Government (2001). *Special Educational Needs and Disability Act.* London: Her Majesty's Stationery Office.

Her Majesty's Government (2015). *Working together to safeguard children: A guide to inter-agency working to safeguard and promote the welfare of children.* Available: www.gov.uk/government/uploads/system/uploads/attachment_data/file/419595/Working_Together_to_Safeguard_Children.pdf (accessed 30 September 2016).

Hinde, J. (1993). Early intervention for alcohol-affected children birth to age three. In J. Kleinfeld and S. Wescott (eds), *Fantastic Antone succeeds!* (pp. 131–149). Fairbanks: University of Alaska Press.

Immordino-Yang, M. and Damasio, A. (2007). We feel, therefore we learn: The relevance of affective and social neuroscience to education. *Mind, Brain and Education Journal*, 1(1): 3–10.

James, C. (2009). *Ten years of family policy: 1999–2009.* London: Family and Parenting Institute.

Karr-Morse, R. and Wiley, M.S. (1997). *Ghosts from the nursery: Tracing the roots of violence.* New York: Atlantic Monthly Press.

Kleinfeld, J. (1993). Conclusion. In J. Kleinfeld and S. Wescott (eds), *Fantastic Antone succeeds!* (pp. 315–322). Fairbanks: University of Alaska Press.

Kleinfeld, J. and Wescott, S. (eds) (1993). *Fantastic Antone succeeds!* Fairbanks: University of Alaska Press.

Laming, LordH. (2003). *The Victoria Climbie Inquiry: Report of an inquiry by Lord Laming.* London: HMSO.

Lewis, I. (2007). Foreword. In *Maternity matters: Choice access and continuity of care in a safe service.* London: Department of Health.

Linnenbrink-Garcia, L. and Pekrun, R. (2011). Students' emotions and academic engagement: Introduction to the special issue. *Contemporary Educational Psychology*, 36: 1–3.

Main, M. and Solomon, J. (1996). Procedures for identifying infants as disorganised/disorientated during the strange situation. In M.T. Greenberg, D. Cicchetti and E.M. Cummings (eds), *Attachment in the pre-school years: Theory, research and intervention* (pp. 121–160). Chicago: University of Chicago Press.

Marmot, M. (2010). Fair society, healthy lives: The Marmot Review. *Strategic Review of Health Inequalities in England post-2010.* Online (accessed 21 September 2016).

May, P.A., Fiorentino, D., Gossage, P.J., Kalberg, W.O., Hoyme, E.H., Robinson, L.K., Coriale, G., Jones, K.L., del Campo, M., Tarani, L., Romeo, M., Kodituwakku, P.W., Deiana, L., Buckley, D. and Ceccanti, M. (2006). Epidemiology of FASD in a province in Italy: Prevalence and characteristics of children in a random sample of schools. *Alcoholism: Clinical and Experimental Research*, 30(9): 1562–1575.

May, P. and Gossage, J.P. (2011). Maternal risk factors for fetal alcohol spectrum disorders: Not as simple as it might seem. *Alcohol Research & Health*, 34(1).

Meins, E. (1997). *Security of attachment and the social development of cognition.* Hove, UK: Psychology Press.

Meins, E. and Fernyhough, C. (1999). Linguistic acquisitional style and mentalising development: The role of maternal mind-mindedness. *Cognitive Development*, 14: 363–380.

Meins, E. and Fernyhough, C. (2006). *Mind-mindedness coding manual.* Unpublished manuscript. Durham University, Durham, UK.

Moore, T.G. (2008). *Early childhood intervention: Core knowledge and skills*. CCCH Working Paper 3. Parkville, Victoria, Australia: Centre for Community Child Health.

Mukherjee, R.A.S. (2013). Fetal alcohol spectrum disorders: Diagnosis and complexities. In B. Carpenter, C. Blackburn and J. Egerton (eds), *Fetal alcohol spectrum disorders: Interdisciplinary perspectives* (pp. 161–173). London: Routledge.

Mukherjee, R., Hollins, S., Abou-Saleh, M. and Turk, J. (2005). *BMJ* (online) 330(7488): 375–376.

Munro, E. (2011). *The Munro Review of Child Protection: Final report: A child-centred system*. Department for Education. London: The Stationery Office.

Murphy Paul, A. (2010). *Origins: How the nine months before birth shape the rest of our lives*. London: Hay House.

National Neonatal Audit Programme (2015). *Annual report on 2014 data*. Available: www.rcpch.ac.uk/improving-child-health/qualityimprovement-and-clinical-audit/national-neonatal-audit-programme-nnap (accessed 8 August 2016).

NOFAS-UK (2010). *Alcohol in pregnancy: Information for midwives*. London: NOFAS-UK.

Page, A., Gayson, C., Vanes, N., Ashmore, P. and McDonnell, A.A. (2016, in press). Sensing what's important: Determining parental preferences of children with Hunters syndrome/Sanfilippo syndrome for when they are receiving treatment in hospital. *RCNi Journal: Learning Disability Practice*.

Page, J. and Elfer, P. (2013). The emotional complexity of attachment interactions in nursery. *European Early Childhood Education Research Journal*, 21(4): 553–567.

Papatheodorou, P. and Moyles, J. (2009). *Learning together in the early years: Exploring relational pedagogy*. London: Routledge.

Popova, S., Lange, S., Shield, K., Mihic, A., Chudley, A.E., Mukherjee, R.A.S., Bekmuradov, D. and Rehm, J. (2016). Comorbidity of fetal alcohol spectrum disorder: A systematic review and meta-analysis. *The Lancet*, 387(10022): 978–987.

Portales-Casamar, E. et al. (2016). DNA methylation signature of human fetal alcohol spectrum disorder. *Epigenetics & Chromatin*, 9(25). DOI: 10.1186/s13072-016-0074-4

Rampage, C., Eovaldi, M., Ma, C. and Weigel-Foy, E. (2003). Adoptive families. In F. Walsh, *Normal family processes: Growing diversity and complexity*. New York: The Guildford Press.

Robertson, C. and Messenger, W. (2010). Early childhood intervention in the UK: Family, needs, standards and challenges. *International Journal of Early Childhood Special Education*, 2(2): 161–171.

Rogoff, B. (2003). *The cultural nature of human development*. Oxford: Oxford University Press.

Rose, J., McGuire-Snieckusa, R. and Gilbert, L. (2015). Emotion coaching: A strategy for promoting behavioural self-regulation in children/young people in schools: A pilot study. *The European Journal of Social and Behavioural Sciences*, XIII: 1766–1790.

Russell, P. (2013). Foreword. In B. Carpenter, C. Blackburn and J. Egerton (eds), *Fetal alcohol spectrum disorders: Interdisciplinary perspectives*. London: Routledge.

Sargeant, A. (2010). *Working within child and adolescent mental health inpatient services: A practitioner's handbook*, edited by C. Barrett. Wigan, UK: National CAMHS Support Service.

Shaughnessy, J. (2012). The challenge for English schools in responding to current debates on behaviour and violence. *Pastoral Care in Education: An International Journal of Personal, Social and Emotional Development*, 30(2): 87–97.

Shortt, J.W., Stoolmiller, M., Smith-Shine, J.N., Eddy, J.M. and Sheeber, L. (2010). Maternal emotion coaching, adolescent anger regulation, and siblings' externalizing symptoms. *Journal of Child Psychology and Psychiatry*, 51(7): 799–808.

Siraj, I., Kingston, D. and Melhuish, E. (2015). *Assessing quality in early childhood education and care: Sustained shared thinking and emotional well-being scale for 2–5 year old provision*. London: Institute of Education.

Siraj-Blatchford, I., Sylva, K., MuttockS., Gilden, R. and Bell, D. (2002). *Researching effective pedagogy in the early years*. Department for Education and Skills Research Report 365.

Skinner, B.F. (1968). *The technology of teaching*. New York: Appleton-Century-Crofts.

Streissguth, A., Clarren, S. and Jones, K. (1985). Natural history of the fetal alcohol syndrome: A 10 year follow-up of eleven patients. *The Lancet*, 2: 85–91.

Streissguth, A. and Kanter, J. (eds) (1997). *The challenge of fetal alcohol syndrome: Overcoming secondary disabilities*. Seattle, WA: University of Washington Press.

Tucker, C.M., Zayco, R.A., Herman, K.C., Reinke, W.M., Trujillo, M. and Carraway, K. (2002). Teacher and child variables as predictors of academic engagement among low-income African American children. *Psychology in the Schools*, 39: 477–488.

United Nations Educational, Scientific and Cultural Organization (UNESCO) (1994). *The Salamanca statement and framework for action on special needs education*. Salamanca.

United Nations General Assembly (1989). *Adoption of a Convention on the Rights of the Child* (UN Doc.A/Res/44/25). New York: UN General Assembly.

United Nations Treaty Collection, Convention on the Rights of Persons with Disabilities (2006). Available: http://treaties.un.org/Pages/ViewDetails.aspx?src=TREATY&mtdsg_no=IV-15&chapter=4&lang=en (accessed 22 October 2012).

Vygotsky, L. (1983). *Thought and language*. Massachusetts Institute of Technology.

Warren, K.R., Hewitt, B.G. and Thomas, J.D. (2011). Fetal alcohol spectrum disorders: Research challenges and opportunities. *Alcohol Research and Health*, 34(1): 4–14.

Weare, K. and Gray, G. (2003). *What works in developing children's emotional and social competence and wellbeing?* Nottingham: DfES.

Webster-Stratton, C. and Reid, M.J. (2004). Strengthening social and emotional competence in young children: The foundation for early school readiness and success. *Infants and Young Children*, 17(2): 96–113.

Whitebread, D. and Bingham, S. (2011). *School readiness: A critical review of perspectives and evidence*. Occasional paper No. 2. Association for the Professional Development of Early Years Educators (TACTYC)/University of Cambridge.

Whitehurst, T. (2010). *Making sense of FASD: Parenting a child with foetal alcohol spectrum disorder*. Unpublished thesis for MSc Clinical Neuropsychiatry, University of Birmingham, School of Medicine.

Young, S., Absoud, M., Blackburn, C., Branney, P., Colley, B., Farrag, E., Fleisher, S., Gregory, G. Gudjonsson, G., Keira, K., O'Malley, K., Plant, M., Rodriguez, Al, Ozer, S., Inyang, T., Woodhouse, E. and Mukherjee, R. (2016). Guidelines for identification and treatment of individuals with attention deficit/hyperactivity disorder and associated fetal alcohol spectrum disorders based upon expert consensus. *BM Psychiatry*, 16: 324. Available: https://bmcpsychiatry.biomedcentral.com/articles/10.1186/s12888-016-1027-y

Index

Page numbers in *italics* indicate figures; page numbers in **bold** indicate tables.

aboriginal populations 9, 30
abuse: ECPs' knowledge of 26, 60; and FASD 31; focus on EI 29; places development at risk 30; PUP programme 32; sexual abuse 14, 15; *see also* child protection; safeguarding
addictions 3, 8, 17, 31
adoption: aboriginal populations 9; case study 18–19; challenges 17; high numbers of FASD children 10, 34n1; need for sensitivity 12–13, 18, 41, 61
adults: adult engagement scale 44; relationship with infants 27, 38, 39–41, 49n1; role in ECD 37–39; scaffolding 38, 46, 47–48; *see also* parents
aggression 4, 15
alcohol consumption: binge drinking 10; consumption statistics 32; information/advice about 11, 32, 33, 59, 61; problematic/dependent drinkers 31; range of health problems 10–11; social justice issue 9; *see also* prenatal exposure to alcohol (PEA)
Alcohol in Pregnancy – Training for Midwives Project 32
alcohol-related birth defects 3, 8, **8**, 9
alcohol-related neurodevelopmental disorders 3, 8, **8**, 30
All Party Parliamentary Group on FASD 31, 59
Allen, Graham 28–29
animal research 3
anxiety: in FASD children 41, 58; result of heavy drinking 10
assessment techniques: Development Matters 43; Early Support Developmental Journals 43; Early Support Materials 43, 57; engagement approach 43–44; sensory preferences 42–43, 49n2, 55, 62; Strengths and Difficulties Questionnaire 44; transdisciplinary assessment 53

attachment theories/issues: attachment and relational theory 39–41; challenges of adoption 17; key worker concept 39; 'secure' attachment 49n1
attention deficit hyperactivity disorder 3, 9, 53
Australia: aboriginal populations 9, 30; lack of FASD knowledge 4
autism 9, 33, 49n2
Aynsley-Green, Sir Al 10

behaviour management: behaviour modification 41; pedagogical approaches 45–46; specialist advice 41
behavioural problems: aboriginal populations 9; attachment difficulties 41; effects of PEA 2, 8, 42; in infancy 3; poor emotional competence 47; response of ECPs 53
binge drinking 10
bio-psychosocial theory 35–37, *36*, 45, 49, 65
birth defects 1, 3, 8, **8**, 9
birth mothers 3, 13–17; *see also* families
birth weight 3, 9, 10
Blair, T. 22
blogs 19
body movements 42
Bowlby, J. 39
brain development: effects of PEA 8, 10, 41; importance of early years 28, 29
breast-feeding 61
Bronfenbrenner, U. 35–37, 43, 49, 65
Bruner, J. 38, 47

case studies: adoption 18–19; birth mothers 13, 14–17
central nervous system 8, **8**
charities 31, 32, 48, 59
Chasnoff, I.J. 41, 45
child protection 12, 26–27, 29–30, 31, 41, 60
Childcare Act (2006) 23, 26

Children and Adolescent Mental Health Services 52
Children and Families Act (2014) 4, 23–24
children's centres 4, 22, 28
chronic serous otitis media 2
circle activities 46, 52, 54, 55, 57
Circle of Hope 19
codes of practice: SEN Code of Practice 4, 22, 23; SEND Code of Practice 23, 24–25
comic strips 47
communication skills: assessment of 53, 60; attachment theories 38, 39; broad area of SEN 25; of ECPs 56; EYFS prime learning area 41; impact of sanctions 41; social stories 47, 52, 55
communities: bio-psychosocial theory 36; community-based services 62; tolerance/understanding 4, 9, 64
Complex Learning Difficulties and Disabilities Project 2, 56
conception 30
conduct disorder 2
congenital anomalies 2, 8
consumption of alcohol see alcohol consumption; prenatal exposure to alcohol (PEA)
Convention on the Rights of Persons with Disabilities 4, 27
Convention on the Rights of the Child 4, 22, 27, 61
counselling services 60, 62
criminal behaviour 4, 10

depression 3, 10, 12, 40
Development Matters 43
developmental milestones 12, 26–27, 40; see also early child development (ECD)
diagnosis of FASD: aboriginal populations 9; complex and multi-faceted 19; diagnostic tools 61; lack of/long delays in 14; need for early diagnosis 9, 10, 32, 62; role of ECPs 54
disabilities: definition 23; intellectual 8, 8, 27; neurological 42; Rights of Persons with Disabilities 4, 27; secondary 8, 9, 13, 30–31, 32; SEND policies 22–27
discrimination 22, 25, 26
drugs: illegal 2, 14, 31, 40, 41; prescribed 2

early child development (ECD): benefits of ECI 27; bio-psychosocial theory 35–37, 36, 45, 49, 65; emotion coaching 46–47, 55; multiple influences on 1, 30, 45; and parenting 28–29; pedagogical approaches 45–46, 47–48; risk factors 1–4; role of adults 37–39; see also attachment theories
early childhood intervention (ECI): benefits 4, 27; challenges 59; distinct from EI 29;

government reviews 27–29; within multiple contexts 37; preventative measures 30, 31; relationship-based services 62–65, 64; role of organisations 31–33; suggested approaches 60–62
early childhood policy: prioritised by governments 21–22; SEND policies 22–27
early childhood professionals (ECPs): Children and Families Act 23–24; EYFS themes 51–58; influence on ECD 37, 41; paucity of knowledge 4–5, 13, 59; professional caregiving 63; professional development 23, 60–61, 64; qualifications/training 26, 33; relationship with families 12–13, 27, 62, 63; SEND CoP 23, 25; see also interdisciplinary practices
Early Education 43
early intervention (EI) 22, 23, 36; and child protection 29–30
Early Intervention Foundation 29, 57
Early Support Developmental Journals 43
Early Support Materials 43, 57
Early Support Programme 22
Early Years Educator 33
Early Years Foundation Stage (EYFS): communication skills 41; developmental assessments 23, 26–27; enabling environments 51, 55–57; key points 26; learning and development 51, 57–58; positive relationships 51, 54–55; socio-emotional development 41; Statutory Framework requirements 43; uniqueness of children 51, 52–53
Early Years Teacher 33
Education, Health and Care plans 24
education/information programmes 19–20, 31–32, 61
emotion coaching 46–47, 55
emotional development see socio-emotional development
engagement approach 43–44
Enhanced Midwifery Service 33
environmental pollutants 2
epigenetics 3, 5n1, 6n2
Equality Act (2010) 25–26
European FASD Alliance 19
Every Child Matters 23
Excellence for All Children: Meeting Special Educational Needs 22
expressive language disorder 2, 12

facial anomalies 8, 8, 19
families: as diverse groups 60; influence on child's development 30, 62; relationships with ECPs 12–13, 27, 62, 63; see also adoption; birth mothers; foster care
FASD organisations 19–20, 31–32

feeding problems 3, 11, 12, 18, 53
Fetal Alcohol Spectrum Disorders (FASD):
    coexisting conditions 2, 19, 53; ECPs' paucity
    of knowledge 4–5, 13, 59; non-genetic cause
    of disability 9; organisations 19–20, 31–32;
    prevalence rates 7; range of conditions 8–9,
    8, 58; scenario of child with FASD 5;
    screening for ADHD 3; strengths/difficulties
    of children 11–12, 44–45; see also prenatal
    exposure to alcohol (PEA)
fetal alcohol syndrome 8, 8
fetus: early brain development 29; effects of
    teratogens 1–3, 7–8, 10, 41; need for
    ECI 30, 31
Field, Frank 28
foster care: aboriginal populations 9; high
    numbers of FASD children 10, 34n1; multiple
    placements 10, 34n1, 41, 42, 52; need for
    sensitivity 12–13, 41, 61
funded childcare 12, 24

games 45, 55
genetic factors 3, 35, 37
Glasgow Children's Hospital Charity 32
government policies: call to improve ECI
    services 31; ECI reviews 27–29; focus on
    poverty 21–22; qualifications for ECPs 33;
    SEND policies 22–27
Green Paper on SEND 22
group activities 45, 48, 54, 55, 57
growth deficiencies 9
guilt 13, 15, 18, 62

health inequalities 27–28
health screening 3, 32–33, 60, 62
hearing impairments 8, 58
herbal medications 2
Hospital Alcohol Liaison Service 32
human rights treaties 4, 22, 27, 61
humanist approaches 41
hyperactivity 8, 12, 42, 44, 55; ADHD
    3, 9, 53

infants: common FASD problems 3, 11–12;
    crucial developmental stage 27, 29; macro
    sociocultural environment 37; relationships
    with adults 27, 38, 39–41, 49n1
information/education programmes 19–20,
    31–32, 61
Inquiry framework for learning 44, 56
insecurity 39, 40, 41
intellectual disabilities 8, 8, 27
interdisciplinary practices: assessment/
    monitoring 26, 61; EYFS context 53, 54;
    pedagogical approaches 63, 64; range of
    professionals 48–49, 48

language development 3, 21, 28, 38, 39, 48
language problems 2, 8, 12, 53
lead 2
learning difficulties 2, 10, 23
legislation: Childcare Act 23, 26; Children and
    Families Act 4, 23–24; Equality Act 25–26;
    Special Educational Needs and Disability
    Act 22
Life Changes Strategy 29
local authorities: and child protection 29; EIF
    programmes 29; legislative requirements 23,
    24; provision of services 62

MAMA Pathway 32–33
Marmot, Sir Michael 27–28
maternal alcohol consumption see prenatal
    exposure to alcohol (PEA)
Maternal Alcohol Management Algorithm
    (MAMA)Pathway 32–33
maternal diseases 2
maternal sensitivity 38–39, 40–41
medications 2
memory loss 5, 8, 10, 30
mental health problems: broad area of SEN 25;
    from heavy drinking 10; perinatal mental
    health 29; provision of services 52, 62; as
    secondary disability 8, 9, 13, 32
mercury 2
microcephaly 9
midwives 13, 31, 32–33
mind-mindedness 37, 38–39, 44
miscarriages 2, 11
motor coordination 42
Mukherjee, Raja 32
Munro, Eileen 29

National Health Service 32
National Organisation on Fetal Alcohol
    Syndrome 19
nervous system abnormalities 2, 8, 8
neurobehavioural problems 2, 3
neurodevelopmental disorders 3, 8, 8, 30
neurological disabilities 42
New Labour 21, 22
NOFAS organisations 19, 31, 32
noise levels 56, 62

organisations (FASD) 19–20, 31–32
outcomes, ECI services 64

parents: and ECI 28–29; EYFS call for
    involvement 26, 54, 57; parent-child
    relationships 3–4, 30, 54, 62, 63, 64; see also
    adults
Parents Under Pressure (PUP) programme 32
partial fetal alcohol syndrome 8, 8

passports *see* sensory stimuli: sensory passports/profile
pedagogical approaches 45–46, 47–48, 63, *64*
peer mentoring 19, 20, 31–32, 62
perinatal mental health 29
photographs 54, 55, 56
physical contact 14, 53
pictures 55, 56
play times: assessments by ECPs 37, 61; favourite activities 52; must be inclusive 54; must be structured 56; promote developmental outcomes 48; social interaction difficult 53; strengths/difficulties 11–12, 55, 57
pollutants 2
postnatal depression 40
poverty: and ECI 28; government concerns 21–22; and health inequalities 27–28; links with SEND 23
pregnancy: fetal brain development 8, 10, 29, 41; foundation for health/well-being 28, 29–30; information/education programmes 61; risks for future pregnancies 56; *see also* prenatal exposure to alcohol (PEA)
premature births: case study 18; and developmental milestones 27; feature of FASD 12; learning problems 10; meeting infants' needs 41; risk factors 2, 11, 52; support for mother 11; UK statistics 10
prenatal exposure to alcohol (PEA): effects on fetus 1–3, 7–8, 10, 41; information/education programmes 61; preference for alcohol after birth 2; risk factors 3; screening via TWEAK 32–33; *see also* alcohol consumption; Fetal Alcohol Spectrum Disorders
pre-school children 6n3, 12, 24
prevalence rates 7
preventative measures 30, 31
Princess Royal Maternity Hospital 32
problem solving 45, 46
professional caregiving 63
professional development 23, 60–61, *64*
professional love 27, 40, 51, 55, 63, *64*
pro-social behaviour 41, 44–46, 47
protection *see* child protection; safeguarding
Public Health 32
puppets 55

qualifications 33
Queen's Speech (2016) 29
questionnaires: Strengths and Difficulties (SDQ) 44; TWEAK 32

receptive language disorder 2, 8, 12
referrals 19, 32, 60
relational theory 39–41
relationship-based ECI 62–65, *64*

Removing Barriers to Achievement 23
risk factors: benefits of ECI 27; future pregnancies 56; PEA/FASD 3; premature births 2, 11, 52; reduced through diagnosis 9, 10
role play 55
routines 12, 56, *64*

safeguarding 26–27, 41, 56, 60
Salamanca Statement on Special Educational Needs 22
scaffolding 38, 46, 47–48
schizophrenia 11
school environment: attachment difficulties 40; and child's early years 28; pre-school children 6n3, 12, 24; scenario of child with FASD 5; time spent learning 43
screening 3, 32–33, 60, 62
secondary disabilities: alcohol/drug addiction 8; mental health problems 8, 9, 13, 32; trans-generational processes 30–31
SEN Code of Practice 4, 22, 23
SENCO 22, 26
SEND policies 22–27; Code of Practice 23, 24–25
sensitivity 38–39, 40–41, 62; in adoption/foster care cases 12–13, 18, 41, 61
sensory processing disorder 42
sensory stimuli: integration of 12, 42, 55, 56, 62; sensory passports/profile 42–43, 49n2, 55
sexual abuse 14, 15
sight *see* vision impairments
skills development *see* communication skills; socio-emotional development
Skinner, B.F. 41
sleeping problems 3, 12
smoking 2, 13, 31
social stories 47, 52, 55
socioeconomic status 3, 7, 11
socio-emotional development: attachment difficulties 40; benefits of ECI 28–29; broad area of SEN 25; emotion coaching 46–47, 55; EYFS prime learning area 41; EYFS strategies 52, 55, 57; infant-caregiver relationship 38; pro-social behaviour 41, 44–46, 47; through playing 48
special educational needs: definition 23; SEND policies 22–27
Special Educational Needs and Disability Act (2001) 22
Special Educational Needs and Disability Code of Practice 23, 24–25
Special Educational Needs Code of Practice 4, 22, 23
special educational provision 23
SSTEW scale 44

stillbirths 11
stories 47, 52, 55
Strange Situation room 39, 49n1
Strengths and Difficulties Questionnaire 44
stress: and attachment difficulties 40; children
    with FASD 58; family/parental stress 21, 30;
    maternal 2, 3
support groups 13, 19, 31–32
Sure Start Children's Centres 4, 6n3
Sustained Shared Thinking and Emotional
    Well-being (SSTEW) scale 44

teachers: engagement approach 43–44;
    qualifications 33; Strengths and Difficulties
    Questionnaire 44; support pro-social
    skills 41
teratogens 1–2, 7
thalidomide 1
Thameside Hospital Maternity
    Service 32
therapy 31, 32, **48**, 61–62
tobacco 2, 13, 31
Together from the Start 22
toys 55

training: FASD organisations 19, 31, 32;
    professional development 23, 60–61, *64*;
    qualifications for ECPs 33; in safeguarding/
    welfare 26
transdisciplinary assessment 53
transition periods 53, 58, 60,
    63, *64*
TWEAK questionnaire 32

UK and European Birth Mum Network 20,
    31–32
UN Convention on the Rights of Persons with
    Disabilities 4, 27
UN Convention on the Rights of the Child 4,
    22, 27, 61

value judgements 13
video blogs 19
violence 4, 10, 30
vision impairments 8, 58
Vygotsky, L. 38

welfare issues 26–27, *36*; *see also* child
    protection; safeguarding

Printed in Great Britain
by Amazon